Elux

ENCOURAGEMENT

for motherhood

A 30 Day Devotional
by Women for Women

Dedication

Lo, children are an heritage of the LORD: and the fruit of the womb is his reward. - Psalm 127:3

To my wonderful children, Tre, Cherish, Lincoln, and Felicity. You are the gifts from God that I have prayed for since I was child.

Tre, your will to do what is right, Cherish your love for Jesus, Lincoln your thrill for life and Felicity your quick wit coupled with your fun personality, are all things that make you each unique and special!

I'm so thankful God has allowed me be your mom! Keep loving and serving Jesus!

You're all my favorite!

Love,
Mom

Praise for
Encouragement From Women Who've Been There

I am a firm believer that sometimes all a person needs is a little bit of hope. Hope that we will make it. Hope that things won't always be the way they are today. We need to know we aren't the only ones experiencing difficult things of all flavors. We need to hear how God's grace has been sufficient in other people's situations, and realize once again that He will be sufficient in ours. We need to know we are not alone. EFW provides just those things. I have been challenged and encouraged as I've gotten glimpses into other ladies' journeys. One of our responsibilities as a Christian is to encourage one another. These devotionals are an avenue of hope, and some days that's all we need!

Joy Lewis
Ministry wife for 28 years, Mother of 5, Grandmother of 1, Ladies Conference speaker, teacher, coach, retreat host, pianist. Founder of *Only God Ministries.*
Somerville, Alabama

One of the highest callings that God has given to women is that of motherhood. Each season of this incredible journey is unique with its own challenges and difficulties. Having other women who have walked this path before me and speak truth into my heart is a source of comfort and joy. As the title suggests, this book will encourage you and refresh your soul.

Robyn McCormick
Co-Founder/Lead Pastor's wife of New Life Baptist Church, Homeschool mom of 5, Grandmother to 1.
Casa Grande, Arizona

All of us women need encouragement! Especially Moms! It is so easy to get bogged down with the monotony of doing the same things over and over everyday that after awhile, it seems useless. We tend to believe we are getting nowhere with our teaching, disciplining, or even our loving. We lose sight of the fact we probably are doing one of the most important jobs in the world. We need to be encouraged! What better way than learning from other godly women who have been there and understand? May the Lord use these devotionals to encourage you and give you a proper perspective of the wonderful job God has given YOU!

Becky Patterson
Missionary to Mexico since 1974, Co-Founder of Iglesia Bautista Monte Abarim, Mother of 5, Grandmother to 12. Arlington, Texas

God uses the right words at just the right times. "Encouragement For Women Who've Been There" is a treasury of wisdom from gracious and godly friends who walk with us on our journey. You will be refreshed to hear from ladies who face similar challenges and carry similar burdens to those you face everyday.

Dana Schmidt
Lead Pastor's wife Emmanuel Baptist Church. Newington, Connecticut

Motherhood is the hardest and yet most rewarding ministry that we will ever have. One of the great gifts from our Sovereign Father is that we don't have to go on the journey alone. We can learn from so many around us. That is exactly what this devotional has done for us. Titus 2:4 says "That they may teach the young women to be sober, to love their husbands, to love their children." Compiled here is wisdom from so many moms who have gone through or are going through what we are facing. Motherhood doesn't need to be lonely- our comfort is the Father and our guide is His letters to us. Our job now is to take the wisdom that we have learned from these women of God and allow it to shape us into the moms God designed us to be. Don't read this devotional in vain, take the wisdom and go on your motherhood journey with confidence that you are the exact person God designed to raise the children He has placed in your arms.

Jackie Teis
Co-Founder, Life Factors Fatherless Ministries, lifefactors.org. Las Vegas, Nevada

EFW fulfills 2 Corinthians 1:4 in away that few ministries can. For many women, it often seems like half the battle is just knowing you are not alone. A good portion of the other half is learning from those who can say "I've been there, done that"; or "I am there doing that." EFW provides both! The insight and true encouragement provided based on biblical wisdom and personal growth found through God's guidance in a variety of life's situations shared by those who have experienced it is a blessing to those most in need.

Aresia Watson, PhD
College professor. Pensacola, Florida

Special thanks to:

Dan Kane - Editor

Heather Cusumano – Cover Design

Table of Contents

Introduction

Dear Exhausted Mom,

It has been said that being a mom is the most rewarding job in the world, but often when we are in the midst of "mothering" and all its "glory," it doesn't feel very rewarding.   At times, it can feel lonely, isolated and down right depressing, but it doesn't have to be that way.

We at Encouragement From Women Who've Been There (EFW) know the great value God places on motherhood and we've experienced both the highs and the lows of what comes along with this special season of life.

If you're a new mom, a single mom, a stepmom or even a grandma, you're going to be encouraged by what you read in the pages of this book. It is my prayer that God uses this book to encourage your heart knowing that the rewards of mothering, and mothering well, can be eternal.

Love in Christ,
Charity

Week One

ENCOURAGEMENT FROM WOMEN

| DAY 1 |

On Loan from God
Charity Joy Berkey

The aged women likewise, that they be in behaviour as becometh holiness, not false accusers, not given to much wine, teachers of good things; That they may teach the young women to be sober, to love their husbands, to love their children, To be discreet, chaste, keepers at home, good, obedient to their own husbands, that the word of God be not blasphemed. - Titus 2:3-5

My children and I often checkout books, movies and CDs from our local Library. It pains me that my children aren't always as careful as they should be with the items on loan. We've returned scratched disks, books with torn jacket covers, and one time we even misplaced a DVD for over a year and a half. One librarian assured me that this is a common occurrence with returned children's item.

Even though they've been instructed on how they should properly handle these borrowed items, my children fail to understand the concept of "replacement cost." The library requires payment for lost movies, usually about $30. Since my children didn't pay the replacement cost of the misplaced movie, they don't value it like the owner would.

I've been thinking a lot lately about the fact that we don't own our children. They are on loan to us from the Lord. With this realization I stumbled onto the notion that the spouse that God gave me is also on loan from

God.

Christ Jesus places a high value on my children and my husband because He paid the ultimate price for each of them. I love my husband and children more than anything in this world, but I've never had to pay a high price for them. God has loaned them to me. He has allowed me, at least for a time, to borrow His precious purchase. He's given me the Holy Spirit to help guide me on how to properly care for each of them because He cares for them even more than I do.

If we don't properly instruct, train and love our children, we are doing a disservice to their Owner. When we think of ourselves before we think of our spouses, we're not just being selfish, we're showing God that we don't treasure this precious gift He has given us.

I'm sometimes guilty of treating my family as used, borrowed library books instead of the invaluable gifts they are. Oh, I care for them. I make sure everything is provided for them, but how easy it is to be frustrated and angry at their childish ways instead of loving, training and properly disciplining them.

I've found that my greatest help in this area is having older, wiser, godly women to whom I can go to for advice, mentors that I can be honest with about my shortcomings. These women don't judge or condemn me for my failures, but they listen. They share with me their own experiences and they point me back to Jesus. I'm so grateful for these women in my life. They would be the first to say that they are not perfect, they are still learning and they will never have it all figured out. But these women are definitely the kind of women Paul wrote to Titus about when he was in Crete. The older women are willing to teach the younger women and the younger women are willing to listen, learn and apply what they learn. This is how God prepares and sustains us to care for His borrowed treasures.

Daily Tip: Find a mentor, maybe your pastor's wife, an older women in the church, one who has proven to be faithful. Be willing to be open and honest so God can use her to truly help you.

Recalculating
Francie Taylor

Be ye followers of me, even as I also am of Christ. - 1
Corinthians 11:1

Our children were in Bible college before my late
husband and I realized that we needed to go back to the
Lord and allow Him to edit our parenting. We were
copycat parrots, not parents. God wanted us to parent
the three precious souls entrusted to us with our eyes
focused on His Word and our souls yielded to His
guidance. We were racing through the child training
years with a misplaced focus. We not only missed the
mark on teaching our children why we did what we
did, but we also had a lack of concentration on our own
godliness. Living in the fast lane can easily lead to the
wrong road.

1 Corinthians 11:1 makes this bold statement: "Be ye
followers of me, even as I also am of Christ." Our lives
said, "Just copy us and follow our directions." We
meant well, but neither of us was raised in a home with
Christ and the Bible as the source of life, so we were
doing a lot of guessing, a lot like driving with a
malfunctioning GPS. We were heading somewhere, but
the route was unclear.

When we're driving in an unfamiliar area, the GPS
helps to guide us and will recalculate if we make a
wrong turn. Parenting is actually a lot like driving into
the unfamiliar, and God is waiting to guide us if we're

willing to listen. Let's consider a few wrong turns and do some recalculating.

Wrong turn: Overreacting to situations that we don't like.

Recalculating: Pause before responding, especially when things have gone wrong, and even more so if you're irritated. It is so easy to overreact, but responding wisely takes a pause.

Plan: We already know that life is unpredictable. Plan to handle matters wisely and then follow the plan when things go off script. *He that handleth a matter wisely shall find good: and whoso trusteth in the LORD, happy is he.* Proverbs 16:20

Wrong turn: Pridefully refusing to admit when we're wrong.

Recalculating: When we're wrong, asking forgiveness promptly keeps us from trying to rationalize. Committing offenses without apologizing sincerely is not only setting a prideful example, it also sows seeds of bitterness. It is sometimes hard for parents to see themselves as wrong, but we can and do make mistakes.

Plan: Purpose now that you will apologize as often as necessary. "But they were wrong, too!" says our pride, trying to keep us from doing the right thing. Resist the urge to defend yourself. *A brother offended is harder to be won than a strong city: and their contentions are like the bars of a castle.* Proverbs 18:19

Wrong turn: Failing to acknowledge that people can and will do wrong, even when they're saved.

Recalculating: When someone has committed an offense against a child, staging a coverup is dishonest, deceitful, and confusing. We may be causing a breach in our relationship with our children, especially if our child was wronged by a person that they should have been able to trust.

Plan: Hard but honest conversations are required when someone has violated Scripture. Call an offense by its name: sin. Otherwise, we're creating a culture that is common in the secular world: "Rules for thee, not for me." Honesty is educational and biblical. *Therefore to him that knoweth to do good, and doeth it not, to him it is sin.* James 4:17

Wrong turn: Treating our spiritual lives like items on a "To-Do" list.

Recalculating: We have several Bibles per person, but are we even reading one? We have a church home, but do we treat it like a trip to the dentist — unwanted but essential? We are being observed by not only our children, but by other peoples' children as well. Do our lives teach them anything about worshipping God, or are they just absorbing patterns for how to live stressed out existences with church added on like an accessory?

Plan: Be really mindful about how you model a life of worship to your children. They are taking their cues and developing their attitudes about God, church, Bible study, and prayer from you. Do they see a person who loves the Lord and who is truly seeking His face, or do they see a robotic "church attender" checking off another item on the weekly to-do list? God is not a project, and church is not a task. Here's a beautiful passage to establish purpose in worship: *Give unto the LORD the glory due unto his name: bring an offering, and come into his courts. O worship the LORD in the beauty of holiness: fear before him, all the earth.* Psalm 96:8-9

As our children grow up, we should also continue to grow, following Christ straight into eternity. Without spiritual growth, we're modeling a "You do you" version of Christianity, which leads to confusion. It's human nature to take a few wrong turns. What matters is what we do when God makes it clear that we need to change course. Let God do the recalculating.

Don't You Trust Me?
Emily Sealy

Take therefore no thought for the morrow: for the morrow shall take thought for the things of itself. Sufficient unto the day is the evil thereof. - Matthew 6:34

When my oldest daughter was about 4 years old, she suddenly became terrified of taking a bath. Actually, terrified seems too light of a word. We weren't sure what brought it on, but one night as we were going through our normal routine, she completely freaked out - screaming and climbing out of the tub. Her whole body was shaking and her heart was pounding. It caught me off guard because I had no idea what her problem was. I checked the water. Nope, not too hot. I looked around the tub. There was nothing scary there.

And thus began two weeks of the same thing. I tried everything, but as soon as I would mention "bath" she would start crying hysterically. After a week or so of this, we finally figured out what exactly she was afraid of - the shower head. It was then that I remembered how recently one of my other children had accidentally turned the shower on while she was in the tub.

We got her to the point where she would get in the tub, but only if the water was already in it and the faucet was turned off. But anytime my hand would go near the faucet or knob to turn on the shower, the freaking out would again commence.

It was so frustrating. I didn't know what to do or how to help. We would talk about how the shower is not scary, but I would not turn it on. She would be fine until it was time to get in the tub. If she had even the slightest thought that my hand would move toward the faucet, the screaming would start.

It doesn't sound as frustrating as it was, but I even cried over the situation. I didn't know what to do. I kept praying with and for her, and kept reassuring her that I would NOT turn on the shower!

At one point, I looked her in the eyes as she was crying and said, "Sweetie, Mommy loves you. I have told you I won't turn on the shower. Don't you trust me?"

Later that night, I was laying in my bed, praying for everything that was on my heart. I was praying for my daughter - for the Lord to help me teach her to not be afraid and to trust me.

I was also pouring my heart out to God about a situation my husband and I were in. We had a lot of uncertainty in our lives. We had taken a huge step of faith regarding our future, and there were many details that were very unclear. And I was scared. I just wanted to know what was going to happen, when everything would come together. I was worried, and I told God all about it.

And then it hit me - like a big ol' knock to the head. It was as if the Lord said to me, "Emily, I love you. I have told you that I will take care of you. Don't you trust me?"

I literally stopped mid-prayer, opened my eyes, and stared into the darkness of my room. Then it hit me. Yes, my daughter had a legitimate fear of the shower. But I felt that we were going through all this for ME to learn this very important lesson.

God has promised in Hebrews 13:5, *...I will never leave thee nor forsake thee.* He says in Jeremiah 29:11, *For I know the thoughts that I think toward you, saith the LORD, thoughts of peace, and not of evil, to give you an expected end.* Philippians 4:19 says, *But my God shall supply all your need according to his riches in glory by Christ Jesus.* Jesus says in Matthew 6:34, *Take therefore no thought for the morrow: for the morrow shall take thought for the things of itself. Sufficient unto the day is the evil thereof.*

I have known these verses for what seems like forever. I have quoted them to friends and family when trying to encourage them. I KNOW these verses. But now, the Lord is asking me to LIVE them.

Here I was, frustrated because I wanted my daughter to trust me, to believe me when I told her I would not do something to harm her. I promised her that. Yet, she would still scream and cry. And that's pretty much what I was doing with God.

He has told me He has His plans, that He has tomorrow taken care of. He knows what's best for me. He is able to take care of it all. And here I am, crying and whining because I am scared and don't know what is going to happen and if we are going to be okay. And God is just wanting me to trust Him.

Let me tell you, I immediately asked God to forgive me for my lack of trust, for not resting our family in His capable hands. I right then and there let our life, future, and family go back into His strong and perfect care. Immediately I felt an overwhelming sense of PEACE flow over me.

Trusting is not an easy thing to do. We are usually so desperate to take matters into our own hands. Then, when we feel everything is completely out of control, we find that stress, heartache, and fear begin to rule our thoughts.
But when we acknowledge that God is in control, and do not allow worry and fear to control our minds, we will feel such a sense of PEACE.

I don't know what is going on in your life. But I ask you now - is God having to ask you, "Don't you trust me?" Take it from me. Just trust Him. You will never regret it. Never.

Oh, and in case you were wondering, my daughter is no longer afraid of the shower. She stopped the screaming episodes just a few days after my giving it all back to God.

Untapped Resources
Heather Cusumano

Rejoice in the Lord alway: and again I say, Rejoice. Let your moderation be known unto all men. The Lord is at hand. Becareful for nothing; but in everything by prayer and supplication with thanksgiving let your requests be made known unto God. - Philippians 4: 4-6

My husband and I were working on our basement and I asked him to build a table for a particular space. The only thing is, he had never built a table before. He didn't know how to start, what to buy, or what tools he would need to complete the project. Though, just as with any project, he diligently began to tap into the resources available to him: YouTube, Lowes, Amazon, studied examples of other tables, etc. Fully utilizing those resources helped my husband effectively build a table that is not only functional, but level, and set on a firm foundation.

Motherhood can be tough. It can feel like we're doing it for the first time…EVERY.SINGLE.DAY. It appears to be everything BUT level and functional. However, God has given three incredible resources to all Believers to help set that level foundation in our homes: The Word of God, the gift of the Holy Spirit, and Prayer. While all three are vital to our daily walk with God, prayer can easily become an untapped resource whose power we underestimate.

Philippians 4: 4-6 gives us a little insight as to how we are to come before God in prayer. Paul encourages us to rejoice….ALWAYS! Not only during the good times, but also in the bad, scary, crazy, and mundane (err…normal). We are to let our gentleness show (ouch…that one hurt) to everyone and not worry about anything because the Lord is near. He goes on to say, we are to make our requests known before the Lord with, and here is one word that can easily and often be overlooked, thanksgiving. The word thanksgiving means thankfulness, or, the giving of thanks. However, it also means gratitude; actively, grateful language to God, as an act of worship.

As a Believer in Christ, we cannot properly come before the Lord with our requests and petitions if we don't first come to Him in thanksgiving. It's a heart attitude.

I love the meme that says something to the effect, "When kids say you never buy them anything," followed by pictures of Christmas bows attached to literally everything: the electrical outlets, the refrigerator stocked full of food, the faucet with running water, the toothpaste, and so on, calling out the many gifts they have greeted with un-thankfulness. Likewise, how often do we go straight to God with all our mom and child(ren)-related problems? How often do we proclaim to Him all the things we need or want without thanking Him for where He has us in that moment? Are we rejoicing in the Lord in such a way that we are actively grateful to God not only for the gift of our child(ren) but the opportunity to be their mother and raise them? A heart of thankfulness helps put our focus on God and takes the focus off ourselves. It leads us into repentance for known sin in our lives (Romans 3:23; 1 John 1:9; Psalm 66:18), and then gives us the ability to ask the God of the Universe for our needs.

To help us better understand how to tap into this gift-of-a-resource, prayer, we have been given insights into Jesus' prayer life through the Gospels (Matthew, Mark, Luke, and John). Notice these three ingredients in His prayers:

1. Consistency (Luke 5:16; Mark 1:32-35)
Jesus was consistent. He prayed throughout His ministry, from beginning to end.

2. Diligence (Matthew 26:36-44; Mark 1:32-35; Luke 5:16, 23:34)
Jesus was diligent. He is recorded in the Bible praying through suffering, in the middle of a trial, and after ministering to the sick and demon-possessed through the night.

3. Selflessness (Luke 11:1-4, 22:32, 23:34; John 17, 17:20; Philippians 2:3-8)
Jesus was selfless. He taught and showed His disciples how to pray. He prayed for the strengthening of others, His disciples, and for God's forgiveness to His enemies.

Jesus' obedience to the Father, and love for others, was the focus of His prayers (Matthew 22:36-40; John 14:15). As moms, our focus ought to reflect that of Jesus': obedience to the Father and loving others (Matthew 22:37-40). Our faithfulness and commitment to the Father through daily devotions (Bible reading, prayer, and Scripture memorization Psalms 1:1-3, 119:11) is key to tapping into the resource of prayer as we bring our petitions for our children before Him.

Prayer is an amazing gift and powerful resource. When we moms are devoted to God, utilizing His resources, and are walking in obedience to Him, He will establish a firm foundation in our homes. Prayer is not to be an underestimated and untapped resource. It is the tool that God will use to build a firm foundation for our homes so they will not be shaken by storms (Matthew 7:24-27).

Cherish the Noise
Jacklyn Gunner

Lo, children are an heritage of the LORD: and the fruit of the womb is his reward. - Psalm 127:3

But when Jesus saw it, he was much displeased, and said unto them, Suffer the little children to come unto me, and forbid them not: for of such is the kingdom of God. - Mark 10:14

It had been a long but good week at our house. Monday, we had gone out for our son's birthday dinner. Tuesday, friends came for dinner. Wednesday was church night, and this particular night our missionary friends were visiting. The kids had done a wonderful job being polite and rolling with the crazy schedule. Plus, they had been in school all week. Not to mention that the next day was my son's sixth birthday, and the cousins were coming to town. So energy was running high and the excitement even higher.

Now picture this—here we were, sitting around the kitchen dinner table and enjoying a great conversation with our missionary friends who were passing through for a few hours. We hadn't seen them in years. We were just catching up and enjoying hearing about all that was going on in their country when suddenly three wild children came running through the kitchen area with superhero masks and capes ready to save the world (probably from each other). They were having the time of their lives!

Now one thing about me: I do not like a lot of noise; it makes my head spin. (How I survive teaching lower elementary and have three children and love it as much as I do, I am not sure!) My husband, on the other hand, is the third of eight children. I believe he could tune out a train coming through the middle of the living room. Why am I telling you this? Well, when the above situation would happen, I would normally tell them it's time to be quiet; we have company, but not this night. I did ask them to go save the world downstairs and not in the middle of the kitchen, but right then I chose to cherish the noise.

A wonderful co-worker reminded me earlier that week that these days will one day pass. The noise will be gone and the house empty. I realized that one day those capes and masks would be traded for phones, sporting events, and time with friends. Only a few short years later, those things would be traded for dorm rooms and keys to their own homes. Children grow and change so quickly. One day my house will be quiet, but not today. I want to cherish the noise more.

Week Two

| DAY 6 |

If I Could Do It Over Again
Sharon Ammons Rabon

That they may teach the young women to be sober, to love their husbands, to love their children. To be discreet, chaste, keepers at home, good, obedient to their own husbands, that the word of God be not blasphemed. - Titus 2:4-5

My husband and I have three married children and seven grandchildren with another one on the way. As I look back on the seasons of our lives, my heart and mind often focus on the days of our family of five. My husband and I both enjoyed every stage of our lives. We enjoyed 4 ½ years before we had children, then, the birth of our first child, second child and then the third. Now, we enjoy family time as a family of 15.

I would do it all over again. It is worth the personal sacrifice! Could we have done a better job of parenting in certain areas? Sure! I look back and see how I could have been stronger and more disciplined in certain areas. My focus in this devotional is not the physical training, but instead the spiritual training. Every child comes to the point of making his or her own decision about living for Christ and doing the right thing. While our children are in our home it is our responsibility to guide them each and every day in their spiritual walks with the Lord.

What are some areas of spiritual guidance that I would do over again?

1. Enjoy a lifestyle of living and doing right.

2. Focus on your children being friends with each other. Playing together should be emphasized and prioritized.

3. Have quality family time each week. That time gets attacked as the children grow so hold on to it while you can. As they get older, don't force it. Just follow your kids to their sports activities, etc. I promise it's worth your time to be a part of their changing and maturing lives. The process of letting go begins early and goes through several seasons that stretch you as a parent.

4. Listen, learn and laugh with your children. You won't regret one second of the time you spent sitting on their beds at night.

5. Have family devotions. Our years of family devotions have molded and changed our family through Bible reading, singing and prayer, as well as good conversation and bonding time. I have many wonderful memories just because of family devotions each night in our home.

6. Make sure that your children have their quiet time with the Lord each and every day. I couldn't change their hearts, but I could make sure that they were reading God's Word. I know that His Word is life changing.

If I could do it over again, I would give just as much of my personal time and energy with no regrets. For those of you with children in your home, have no spiritual regrets! Begin now so that you can say, "If I could do it over again, I would do the same things over again!"

Lessons from a Captive
Sarah Link

Now Naaman, captain of the host of the king of Syria, was a great man with his master, and honourable, because by him the LORD had given deliverance unto Syria: he was also a mighty man in valour, but he was a leper. And the Syrians had gone out by companies, and had brought away captive out of the land of Israel a little maid; and she waited on Naaman's wife. And she said unto her mistress, Would God my lord were with the prophet that is in Samaria! for he would recover him of his leprosy. And one went in, and told his lord, saying, Thus and thus said the maid that is of the land of Israel. - 2 Kings 5:1-4

The first time I remember hearing about the "little maid" I was still just a little girl with a big imagination. Learning the story of this Hebrew girl who had been taken captive out of her homeland and made a servant of Israel's enemy, Syria, always got to me. Her reality tugged at my young heart as I tried to imagine being in her place. Separated from family and living with an enemy. No way would I survive and actually try to help my captors. My young imagination filled in the details of how I thought the story should go and, surely, I would have planned a kung fu style escape and left my captors to writhe in their loathsome leprosy. Ah, my young mind had it all wrong.

I obviously missed the point of that Scripture the first time I heard it as little girl. But this Scripture captured more than my imagination as I grew older. The lesson from her story captured my heart and here's why. When a captive cares enough to point her captor to the healing power of God there are lessons to be learned:

Even those in high positions need the healing power of God.

Great positions hold great power but everyone still needs the healing power of God. In spite of the high position Naaman held, he still got leprosy. He had a painful disease that put him in the awkward position of asking the enemy for help. He came to a time in his life where he needed help and healing. Powerful people don't truly "have it all" until they experience the healing power of God.

Locations change but God doesn't change.

She was no longer at home with her family and her people. She was now a prisoner of war in Syria and forced to be a servant for the wife of the man who was responsible for capturing her.

She could have concluded that God wasn't whom she heard He was because of what He allowed to happen to her. Her actions show that she knew God and that He was still Whom He said He was. A lowly servant girl was able to influence the powerful to be introduced to the most Powerful of all!

Prepare little hearts to believe that God works wonders.

The little girl spoke out of truth what she had already

been taught. She knew that God could do what needed to be done for her captor "Would God my lord were with the prophet that is in Samaria! For he would recover him of his leprosy." I want to teach my children, daily, the powerful truth of who God is and what He can do! The little maid was no longer home but she still spoke of what she had been taught while she was home! That will preach to a parent's heart! We as Christians should live our lives teaching our children biblical truth so when the unexpected happens they will be prepared to do what God wants them to do.

If you read the whole account in 2 Kings 5 the truth the young girl spoke didn't just stay within the walls of where she was captive. It went far. It went to Naaman, it went to the king of Syria, the King of Israel and eventually it got to Elisha the prophet whom God would use to heal Naaman. And today we have it at our fingertips as a constant reminder of what God does with a little girl willing to be used by Him.

Maybe she didn't escape in the way my young imagination thought she should. She actually did so much more. She showed how a captive could show a powerful man God's healing power. Her location may have changed, but her God didn't. And that's so important in preparing little hearts to believe that God works wonders!

Fight for Your Crew!
Nichole Rabon

And these words, which I command thee this day, shall be in thine heart: And thou shalt teach them diligently unto thy children, and shalt talk of them when thou sittest in thine house, and when thou walkest by the way, and when thou liest down, and when thou risest up. - Deuteronomy 6:6-7

I. LOVE. MY. CREW.

And I'll do everything I can to protect them. Sometimes, protection doesn't necessarily look like the picture of Mama bear. Although I'm willing to fight for them, I'm also willing to teach them to fight for themselves.

I'm here to help guard them against evil, but I must teach them to build a guard and defense for themselves.

I'm here to teach and model a life based upon God's Word, but I'll teach them to read it and apply it to their own lives.

I'm here to feed them nutritious meals, but I'll teach them to choose healthy foods on their own.

I'm here to monitor their friendships, but I'll teach them how to be a good friend and separate themselves from the fakes.

Fight for your crew, and fight hard, but also teach them how to fight those fiery darts!

Four Things I Want to Teach My Children
Kaitlyn Gellos

Train up a child in the way he should go: and when he is old, he will not depart from it. – Proverbs 22:6

I don't know about you, but I sometimes find myself mentally bogged down with how MUCH there is to teach my children. They are given to us for this brief window of time, and we have the responsibility to teach them SO many things. If I'm not careful, I can start chasing a lot of rabbits in child training, while missing a great deal of the "big picture."

As mamas, we are human, we are weak, and we are certainly in need of God's working through us to accomplish anything. Here are some things I am praying for God to help me teach my kids…

1. To share Jesus

My greatest desire for my children is that they will be Christ followers and "Christ sharers." The world is turning from Christ to other things at an alarming rate, racing to fill a void that only Jesus can fill. Too many Christians, myself included, are not always faithful in sharing this treasure we have in the Gospel. I pray that my children will be passionate followers of (and witnesses for) Christ. Matthew 9:37 comes to mind, *The harvest truly is plenteous, but the labourers are few.*

2. To work hard

A lot of problems in life can be avoided if one learns the value of hard work. I want my children to know that work is not a negative thing. God created us to work, to serve, to embrace the responsibilities given to us. Life will not go well for a lazy person. And of course, this training starts when children are young. It is easier for me to do all the things myself, especially when it comes to household chores, because I know they will be done to my satisfaction. It takes vigilant effort and patience to teach my children to work willingly and cheerfully.

3. To use their talents and abilities to glorify God

Do children need praise? Yes. LOTS of praise. I am always looking for areas in which to praise them, encourage them, and motivate them. But beyond, "Good effort!" and "You are really doing well with that!" or "What a good helper you are!" I want them to know that God has a special purpose for giving them their strengths, and even their personalities. I want to build them up, while encouraging them to find creative ways to share what they have with others, for Christ's glory.

4. To be humble

Our shining example of humility, as with all good things, is Christ Jesus Himself. ...*He took upon him the form of a servant...,* Philippians 2:7 We are born as selfish individuals. Children and adults alike must live contrary to our very natural (and sinful) desire to be self exalting.

I can still hear my mom reminding my siblings and me

of Proverbs 13:10, *Only by pride cometh contention.* Usually she would quote it (or have us quote it) as we were arguing over some "worthy cause," like the tubes of toothpaste, or whose turn it was to sit in the front seat. Opportunities for teaching moments on surrendering our pride are abundant with young children.

Humility. I want them to learn it's value. As a mama, I can exemplify this biblical quality when I find myself agitated or cross with the children. I can excuse my behavior because, "The kids were misbehaving," or I can humbly ask their forgiveness. *Let nothing be done through strife or vainglory; but in lowliness of mind let each esteem other better than themselves.* - Philippians 2:3

What are some things, with God's help, you want to teach your children?

Imperfectly Perfect
Haley Shoemaker

Then said the LORD unto me, Go yet, love a woman beloved of her friend, yet an adulteress, according to the love of the LORD toward the children of Israel, who look to other gods, and love flagons of wine. So I bought her to me for fifteen pieces of silver, and for an homer of barley, and an half homer of barley. - Hosea 3:1-2

I recently took a photo. It's not a perfect picture, but it's a picture of my little girls having fun and playing with their Dad. And that is perfect for me.

I knew I loved the story of Hosea, but recently it has resonated with me even more. This is the story of a prophet whom the Lord told to take a harlot for a wife. The text says he even had to pay for her. The woman's name was Gomer.

This command seems uncharacteristic at first. However, God then takes this imperfect marriage and created a perfect picture of how Christ was going to buy back Israel back. Ultimately, it is a picture of Christ paying for our sins on the cross.

Hosea's and Gomer's relationship was meant to be an illustration for the Israelites while in their idolatry. God was showing His people that He would give them mercy and fight through the mess of their sin to buy them back.

At this phase of life, messes are all around me at all times. Life is messy. Love is messy. Even though I like things and circumstances to be all neat, tidy, and clean, this is not reality in life or relationships. It often seems that once I have one mess cleaned up, another one has mysteriously appeared somewhere else. I could let frustration get the best of me, and I often have.

It is important to remember in these moments that the tidiness of my home will not matter when I answer for how well I served the Lord as a wife and mother. I could have all the things on my checklist done, or I could pour myself into the lives of my children and my spouse.

One thing I have found in life is that truly beautiful love actually comes about in the midst of difficulty. Love is beautiful when you work through the mess. When you push all of the selfish wants and desires aside, you can truly love.

Even when you are hurt and bruised, if you choose to turn a blind eye to that pain and love rather than lash out, then you have found what it is to truly have a godly love. God worked through the mess of our sin filled lives and reached out to save us even though we were still in rebellion against Him. There is nothing as beautiful as that! The question is: do we then show that same love to the people around us?

Week Three

ENCOURAGEMENT FROM WOMEN

| DAY 11 |

Just Noise
Calah Vogel

Though I speak with the tongues of men and of angels, and have not charity, I am become as sounding brass and tinkling cymbal. - 1 Corinthians 13:1

I can't quite tell you when it happened. Maybe a year ago, maybe 2 months ago, maybe even years ago, and I just didn't notice. But at some point, my children's attitude about school, chores, and normal life got to me! My patience was gone! I wanted immediate obedience, and when it didn't happen I lost all patience, kindness, gentleness, etc.!

I lost all "charity" in my heart! I demanded obedience! I raised my voice! I got tougher and tougher on them! But the crazy thing is, they didn't get any better! Their noncompliance got worse and worse! What was I doing wrong?!? It was as if they didn't even hear me!!

But I was doing everything "right!"

Then the Lord, in His grace, brought me to 1 Corinthians 13:1, *Though I speak with the tongues of men and of angels, and have not charity, I am become as sounding brass and tinkling cymbal.*

That's why my children didn't hear anything I said. Without patience and gentleness, I was nothing but NOISE to them. My heart was broken! I want my children to hear me! I want to have a peaceful and loving relationship with them. I have to change!

Perhaps your situation is different. Perhaps it's a co-worker or a husband who seems not to hear you, or even a friend. Stop and think, "Have I lost all 'charity' towards this person?" Not the world's definition of love! But God's definition!

Charity suffereth long, and is kind; charity envieth not; charity vaunteth not itself, is not puffed up. Doth not behave itself unseemly, seeketh not her own, is not easily provoked, thinketh no evil; Rejoiceth not in iniquity, but rejoiceth in the truth; Beareth all things, believeth all things, hopeth all things, endureth all things. Charity never faileth... - 1 Corinthians 13:4-8a

So how's your charity? Do your family and friends hear you? Or are you just noise?

I'd love to end this devotional and say I've mastered this patience and kindness thing, but I'm still in the middle of applying this practically in my own life. So let's do this together!

Daily Tip: Pray every day for God's divine help! Ask Him to give you everything you need that day to do His will! Ask Him to fill your heart with His love for your husband, children, friends, family, co-workers, and all sinners! I also specifically ask God to keep me connected with the vine (John 15:4-5) and to set a watch before my mouth (Psalm 141:3). And stay in His Word!

Let's not just be noise! But LOVE!

These Newborn Days
Kaitlyn Gellos

Lo, children are an heritage of the LORD: and the fruit of the womb is his reward. - Psalm 127:3

New babies! Can anything compare with the wonder and miracle of new life? We welcomed baby number five into our family a few weeks ago, and are once again amazed, excited, and sleep-deprived.

There is always an adjustment period when a new little person joins the ranks. Suddenly your life as a Mama is consumed with feedings, diapers, trying to find a schedule that will work for baby while meshing with the family's already established schedule, feedings, extra laundry, staring and studying tiny, perfect features, a million kisses, feedings...

And one day you realize that your time with the Lord is not as long, quiet, or consistent as it was before the babies arrived. Don't be discouraged, Mama of littles! Here are a couple of things I want to encourage you with today...

1. God gave you this baby to glorify Himself.

Life is a series of seasons. And God is in control of them all. It is incredible to think that God knew exactly when you would conceive this baby. In His infinite wisdom, He blessed you with a life to bear and birth, and has now equipped you with the ability to care for this little one. In Psalm 127:3 we read that children are an heritage of the Lord, and the fruit of the womb is his reward. Not our reward, because we are deserving. No, babies are HIS reward! To bring Him glory. And He has entrusted us with these rewards.

2. You can worship God through the mundane and messes of motherhood.

Sometimes, we mistakenly allow ourselves to think that unless we are sitting quietly, uninterrupted, with our Bibles open and a notebook in hand, that we are not truly spending quality time with the Lord. When you have a baby, there will not always be a solid, uninterrupted hour (sometimes there may not be an uninterrupted five minutes. Ha!).

-But when you are feeding your baby, you can pray.

-When you are rocking or pacing the floor with your baby, you can sing to her of God's rich mercy, grace, and love.

-As you sit and stare at the perfection of God's handiwork in the form of your child, you can thank Him and praise His goodness.

-Have a Bible app on your phone? You can read a few verses while the baby naps.

-If you don't have a free hand, you can listen to Scripture read aloud.

Dwell on the Scripture when you can. Study in depth

when you can. But realize that worshipping the Savior should be an act that is demonstrated throughout all the day. A relationship with Christ is so much more than a Bible reading checklist. Don't let the exhaustion of these newborn days keep you from having a close relationship with the Lord. You will need Him more than ever now. And He is there, waiting for you. *Draw nigh to God, and He will draw nigh to you* (James 4:8). What a beautiful promise for every phase of life.

Now if you will excuse me, the baby is awake... it's feeding time.

Filling Up the Spice Jars
Jen Helton

I thank my God upon every remembrance of you. -
Philippians 1:3

Today, I was filling up my spice jars and honestly,
although a rather menial task, it made me smile. Here
are the spices I filled:

1. Mustard and red chilies from a dear friend in
Thailand

2. Old Bay into a shaker from Annapolis Pottery
Factory (Shout out to the Marylanders)

3. Paprika into an antique shaker bought in Budapest
when we took our daughter to visit friends for her
senior trip

Now you may be thinking that this has no point except
to explain what is on this weirdo's spice rack but these
spices are symbolic of so much more than that - they
represent memories, loved ones, amazing vacations,
and even sweet reminders of a childhood living on the
Chesapeake Bay. Anyone who knows me or has been to
my home will attest to the fact that I associate
everything with a memory of a person or experience;
from the frames on the wall to the candles on the
shelves. Everything has a memory attached to it! Weird
as it may sound, this comes from something my mother
once told me when I was pregnant with my first child:

"Build memories. They don't cost a thing and last forever."

That advice, although intended as parental, has been an integral part of my family for many years. No amount of money can replace the joy given when recalling a beautiful day at the beach or a laugh at the time our minivan got searched by sniffing dogs on a military base because sarcasm isn't exactly appropriate when talking to military police (true story).

Therefore shall ye lay up these my words in your heart and in your soul, and bind them for a sign upon your hand that they may be as frontlets between your eyes. - Deuteronomy 11:18

The Bible tells us that we should always strive to remember what God has done for us and how He has blessed us. We should reflect God's blessings in our lives and share them with others as a testimony to His all sufficient grace. Now this does not mean we should chuck or forget everything that doesn't bring us joy; it means that we should ponder the moments that God has given us because He has allowed them in our lives according to His plan.

But Mary kept all these things, and pondered them in her heart. - Luke 2:19

The truth is, not all memories are rosy and full of sunshine. There are memories in my home of times that brought pain: the Turkish coffee pot that my husband bought in Iraq after he had been near an IED explosion that now affects his hearing (he claims he doesn't hear high pitched whining) or the surgical screws from one of the operations I have had over the years. These aren't the most pleasant of memories but they are the experiences that God allowed our family to go through under His tender love and care.

And he said unto me, My grace is sufficient for thee: for my strength is made perfect in weakness. Most gladly therefore will I rather glory in my infirmities that the power of Christ may rest upon me. - 2 Corinthians 12:9-10

Although some memories are not so pleasant to reflect upon, God supplies us with a beautiful grace that makes us strong even in the unpleasantness! These may be memories of pain that God has asked us to lay at His feet in order to have healing, or possibly, memories that He uses to remind us of what we were and how far He has brought us! Whatever the case, memories are a integral part of whom we are, or in some cases, whom we are not.

So as you go about your day today, observe the little reminders that God has placed in your life; the messy handprint on the wall from a child, blue paint on the door of a car from a pole in a parking garage (also a true story), a postcard hanging on a cubicle wall. These are reflections of His grace in times of pain and blessings in times of joy. Take time, today, to ponder how truly amazing God is and how far He has brought you. And don't forget to have this time of reflection with a cup of coffee because coffee makes everything better!

| DAY 14 |

Single Mama Squad
Faith Glosser Conaway

My grace is sufficient for thee: for my strength is made perfect in weakness. - 2 Corinthians 12:9

Parenting is HARD! Single parenting multiplies the burden, worry, and exhaustion because all the work rests on one set of shoulders instead of two. Yet it is not a job anyone asked for. We find ourselves in this boat, and our choices are to row or sink. I would love to share a little bit of my heart on this matter; since I believe the more we learn about those around us, the better we can minister to them.

Strength
People tell me all the time how strong I am and that I'm a superhero. While I understand and appreciate this sentiment, I don't always agree. What I have learned is that strength is born of adversity and necessity. You do what you have to do to survive. Being the sole provider physically, emotionally, and spiritually for children as a single mama is tough. We were never meant to bear this burden alone. I do know this for certain though – God has promised to fill in the gaps between my ability and my children's needs. I have seen this over and over and over again.

Support
We cannot do it alone. I sometimes joke about it, but there are many, many times when I need to be in 2, 3, or 4 places at once. My kids are at that age when their

schedules are as full as mine. Sometimes my plate is so full all it takes is one small thing to topple that delicately balanced tower of responsibilities. It may just be a traffic jam or a forgotten gallon of milk or having to stay 10 minutes late at work that throws the whole evening off kilter. I am so grateful to have several people I can depend on to help me when I need a kid picked up, when my lawn mower breaks, when I forgot to turn on my crock pot, or I get a flat tire. Everyone needs such a friend but ESPECIALLY a single mama.

Share
I do not mention this for sympathy; just to open your eyes to a situation that is difficult to understand if you have not been there. Single parenting is a lonely road. Many times I have wanted and needed to share the burdens or highlights of my own day. Wanted to celebrate with someone when my child achieves something difficult. Needed a shoulder to lean on when I felt like I was failing as a parent. I am extremely blessed to have a circle of friends and family who fill these needs for me as much as they can. Maybe you can do this for someone?

Socialize
Single mamas eat, sleep, and breath their kids. It is an all-consuming job that never ends. We need community, and invitations, and companionship! We need to be invited to activities, groups, girls night out, and parties just like couples are. We may have to decline because of time constraints, responsibilities, or lack of spending money, but extend the invitation!

Sounding Board

Making decisions all alone is no fun. Different perspectives, personalities, and wise counsel all contribute to sound decision making. Without a spouse to bounce ideas off of we are often left second-guessing our direction and decisions for our families. I have several trusted friends I reach out to when making big decisions. This may sound simple but it is so essential to making well-rounded, wise choices.

Sensitive
We may look like we have our act together, but underneath that thick skin is a puddle of emotion, stress, and weariness. Sometimes the simple gesture of a hug can make all the difference. Several years ago in church a lady walked up to me and hugged me and said "I was a single mom once and I KNOW you need a hug so every time I see you I am going to hug you." On many Sundays, that hug is the best part of my day. What a small way to meet a need!

Daily Tip:
What can you do? Come along side a single mom and/or her kids. Pray for them! Sit with her at church. Call her to see if she needs to talk. Listen if she bares her soul. Contribute to programs that support the needy. Ask them over for dinner. Invite her kids along on school/summer holidays when she has to work and her kids would otherwise miss out on fun activities. Take pictures of her kids and send them to her when she has to miss a school function that you were able to attend. Teach your kids that her kids are not to be shamed or made to feel less worthy of love and inclusion just because her family may look different than yours. Text her to check up on her. Offer to watch

her small children so she can have a break. Extend a hug. Invite her to girls' night out. Fill her car with gas. Make her feel considered, included, and cared for.

| DAY 15 |

Before You Blink
Charisse Goforth

Whereas ye know not what shall be on the morrow. For what is your life? It is even a vapour, that appeareth for a little time, and then vanisheth away. - James 4:14

Train up a child in the way he should go: and when he is old, he will not depart from it. - Proverbs 22:6

But Jesus called them unto him, and said, suffer little children to come unto me, and forbid them not: for of such is the kingdom of God. - Luke 18:16

This is the day which the LORD hath made; we will rejoice and be glad in it. – Psalm 118:24

As arrows are in the hand of a mighty man; so are children of the youth. Happy is the man that hath his quiver full of them... - Psalm 127:4-5b

Today I babysat all four of my grandchildren. My granddaughters went home but my grandsons spent the night. After a long day, I finally heard the soft breathing of sleeping babies as I tiptoed out of my room and down the hall. I shut the bathroom door and looked up at the Superman PJ's hanging there.

Within seconds my heart rushed back 20 years and I just wanted to hold those PJ's and live in that moment. Does my daughter realize how beautiful this moment in her life is? When she looks at those little PJ's does her heart fill with overwhelming love and thankfulness for having this little Superman in her life? Ethan will never be this age again. A little older every day. Every hour. Time goes by so quickly. I'm sure my daughters both realize this but just like every mom, when you're in the heart of it you feel like it will never end, there will never be a break.

But then you blink.

You blink the tears away on their first day of school. Before you know it you're blinking the tears away as they graduate from high school, as they drive off to college, as they say "I do" to the love of their life.

The laundry that was never ending and the dishes that were never done. The running to and from sporting events. The clothes and toys that didn't get picked up and the beds that didn't get made. The sleepless nights. The times you hid in the bathroom for just 5 minutes of quiet, even though 2 of those minutes little fists were pounding on the door and your name was being called. The never ending constants.

But then you blink.

Suddenly there aren't any more sporting events or dishes or beds that need to be made. And some days you sit in their bedroom thinking that it was just yesterday you were rocking your little superhero to sleep. He was snuggled in your arms whispering his love for you with sleepy eyes and a smile.

Mama of little ones, stop what you are doing. Put your phone down. Look at your babies. Hold them, sing to them, read to them, memorize every thing about their tiny little faces. Don't take one second for granted. Play with them and pray with them, laugh with them, love on them. Just BE with them.

Before you blink.

Daily Tip:
Don't allow the constants of the day to get you down. Remind yourself daily that you are exactly where God wants you in this moment and rejoice in that fact. You are doing HIS work. Cherish each day, no matter what that day holds. Be so very glad that God has given you one more day to make a difference in the lives of your children and always, always thank Him for that.

Week Four

ENCOURAGEMENT FROM WOMEN

| DAY 16 |

What is Love?
Muriel Livermore

Charity suffereth long.... - 1 Corinthians 13:4a

Modern conveniences...did the Starbucks drive thru pop into your mind? Or maybe a microwave? Perhaps your favorite restaurant that does take out? All these things are designed to be convenient for you.

Moms, you know that small thing you created, that you adore, and thank God for giving to you? Yes, your child. The one that walks underfoot, throws up on you in the middle of the night, and yells at you because you won't let him tear open a box of cookies in the store before paying for it? The one that has a clock set for needing to go to the bathroom as soon as you click the last seat belt in the car. The one that wakes up screaming because she sees something on the wall and it's just the lamp's shadow. The one who has special health needs that you pray God would help you and him through because only God knows this child better than you do. The midnight feeds that help pack on the pounds for those adorable chubby cheeks. The cold meals, the exhaustion, the love…

That's right. As mothers, we do what we do for our children because of love. Love is the sacrifice of self for the benefit of others. Love is the fuel that we thrive on to help these little people find a greater Love. You may not be a mother in your current walk of life, but one thing we can all practice doing daily is loving others.

The world literally sings about finding love, being in love, loving others...but what's missing is that supernatural Love that only comes from Christ. This is the love that we need daily in order to not burn out with loving others, especially when it comes to rearing and training our children. The Bible says in 1 John 4:8b ...*God is love*. People, including our children, need the supernatural love that only comes from God.

God's love is explained in 1 Corinthians 13:4a *Charity suffereth long...* that simply put means "Love is patient with the inconvenient." I personally am not a fan of being thrown up on at 3 am by my 2 year old after having had a baby 2 weeks prior. It's rather inconvenient for both me and my husband because he had to stay home from work to care for our sick child while I kept our newborn away. The next part of 1 Cor. 13:4 says ...*and is kind*. In other words, love is patient with the inconvenient, and is kind to the inconvenient. I didn't yell at my boy for getting sick, but there are times, if I'm honest, that I fail at being kind to my kids, especially when they inconvenience me. How can one truly love others if we fail at being kind? Well let's look to the Bible to see what God says we can do.

In Galatians 5:22 God says, *But the fruit of the spirit is love, joy, peace, long-suffering, gentleness, goodness, faith.* When we ask God to fill us with the Holy Spirit (Who is God Himself and God is love), we can display and deliver the supernatural love it requires to truly Love others. When you are filled with the Holy Spirit, God will lead you to display a supernatural love that brings joy and peace into your heart toward the inconveniences caused by those around you.

To whom can you show God's love today?

Daily Tips:

- It is okay to take a refresher and re-ask the Holy Spirit to fill and control you. It's when we are filled with ourselves that we fail to deliver God's love.

- Find someone you can show God's love to today. Be bold and invite them to accept Jesus as their Savior so they can experience true love, too. The world craves true love.

- Meditate on this passage 1 Corinthians 13:4-8 and remember, God is only a prayer away.

| DAY 17 |

Post Them On Your Wall
Katie Oatsvall

Create in me a clean heart, O God; and renew a right spirit within me. - Psalm 51:10

This verse is intentionally on display in my home. It's placed where I can see it every day.

I also taped up a verse on a 3 x 5 card of Proverbs 25:28, *He that hath no rule over his own spirit is like a city that is broken down, and without walls.* I usually come across that when I am angrily banging around in the kitchen, or not having self-control with my tongue.

Since this is a devotional book for encouragement, I want to share something that happened to me recently to encourage you in a simple area.

My 15-month-old son climbed on the back of our heavy kitchen chair and it fell over on top of him. This caused his mouth to bleed, like most mouth injuries do. A lot!

Ever since I've had babies, I get queasy at the sight of blood. I was about to pass out from looking at him and his dangling gum and exposed tooth (too much detail?)!

My head was spinning, or was it the room? I sat down on the kitchen floor because I was holding my son, and I wanted to prepare for a gentler fall! Then, I looked up and saw the verse on my letter board:

When my heart is overwhelmed, lead me to the rock that is higher than I.

In that moment, I felt pretty overwhelmed. But after reading that verse, I was able to calm down. I truly believe that He calmed my spirit! *Thou wilt keep him in perfect peace, whose mind is stayed on Thee: because he trusteth in Thee,* says Isaiah 26:3.

What do I want to encourage? Have verses around your house. In the book of Deuteronomy, the children of Israel were encouraged to write the commandments, statutes and judgments on the posts of their houses, and on their gates. This would aid in teaching them to their children, and to talk about them, and to bring them to the front of their minds (Deuteronomy 6:1-9).

Get some encouraging verse signs that help you redirect your mind back to the Lord Jesus Christ. Write down a verse on a 3 x 5 card that you would like to memorize, and put it right in front of your kitchen sink. We live in a Pinterest world, an Etsy world, and even a Hobby Lobby world! There are many choices out there to help us display Scripture in our homes.

I Still Have a Lot to Live For
Katie Chappell

When Christ, who is our life, shall appear, then shall ye also appear with him in glory. - Colossians 3:4

I was at home with the kids and had just cut the bottle top off of my two year olds bottle top because she was a little too addicted to it.

I cut it off and said, "Oh nooo it's brokennn... let's throw it in the trash!" I was on top of the world and was feeling like a #momboss — I finally conquered the bottle! I sat down to relish my victory when all of the sudden I felt a sharp pain in my stomach and rushed to the bathroom. I threw up once and chalked it up to the flu so I sat back down just feeling crummy and looking very pale!

Flash forward to two hours and I couldn't even walk — I could only crawl. I thought maybe I had appendicitis because when I pushed on my stomach there was pain. I'd soon find out that this pain had nothing to do with my appendix.

I told my husband I needed him to drive me to urgent care but not to worry because I was sure I'd be fine! Shortly after being checked in, the nurse had me take a test to make sure I wasn't pregnant (though I KNEW I wasn't and we definitely were not trying.) In fact, when she said that they needed to do a pregnancy test, I literally replied, "that would be a surprise!" .... Well,

SURPRISE! The test was positive. When the doctor came in, he told me I most likely had an ectopic pregnancy. My heart dropped!

Around this time, my pain was escalating and I noticed that my right shoulder was REALLY hurting. I started to Google the symptom and realized this pain was called referred pain and could be a sign of internal bleeding.

Seven-hour story short, after many tests and passing out in the ER, I found myself getting prepped for emergency surgery. The ectopic pregnancy had caused my right tube to rupture and was causing severe internal bleeding.

At this point, I was having difficulty even breathing. I was starting to get pretty nervous. I couldn't help but think about my incredible husband and my three young kids— not trying to be dramatic, but I really wasn't ready for this life to end. As I was getting wheeled back to the operating room, with a smile I said to the surgeon, "I have a 5 year old, a 3 year old, and a 1 year old... I still have a lot to live for."

Those eight words have been ringing in my ears ever since: I still have a lot to live for.

What am I living for? What are you living for? Take a moment to consider who God has called you to be. What type of friend, mother, daughter, leader? What steps are you taking to bring you closer to that purpose?

If you're like me, those questions can be a bit overwhelming! I recently heard it said that before we worry about what we need to DO we need to be concerned with the WHO. If I know WHO I want to become, the DO will follow.

Allow me to explain... I've always known who I want to be, but the stress of becoming that person, at times, almost feels like too big of a task. I want to be a godly woman who knows the Bible inside and out, a woman who leads others to Christ, a loyal friend, a wife who makes my husband proud, and a mother to whom my daughters can aspire to be all the while teaching my son how to be strong and kind.

So, if I know that I want to become someone who knows the Bible inside and out, I should dive into the Bible more frequently. The Bible says in 2 Timothy 2:15, *Study to shew thyself approved unto God, a workman that needeth not to be ashamed, rightly dividing the word of truth.*

If I know I want to be a mom whom my kids can look up to, I will speak kindly to them and show them the love of Jesus. Deuteronomy 11:19 says, *And ye shall teach them your children, speaking of them when thou sittest in thine house, and when thou walkest by the way, when thou liest down, and when thou risest up.*

You get the point! I need to start with the WHO and let the DO overflow from the WHO. (Kind of sounds like a Dr. Seuss rhyme).

I still have a lot to live for. Mainly because I have yet to live up to whom I was created to become. I am so thankful for the opportunity to live and I thank God every day for the precious life he has given me. The Bible says in Colossians 3:4, *When Christ, who is our life, shall appear, then shall ye also appear with him in glory.*

Christ IS my life, which in turn motivates me to share His life-giving and life-changing message! What an honor!

You have a purpose and you still have a lot to live for! So get out there and be who you were created to become.

When I think back to that eventful day in the hospital I am reminded that in life and loss, God's love endures forever. We look forward to meeting our tiny trouble-maker someday and are thankful for a God who heals.

PS- Guess who has her bottle back? #momfail

To Battle With Your Kids or Battle for Your Kids
Laurie McCann Billings

Arise, cry out in the night: in the beginning of the watches pour out thine heart like water before the face of the Lord; lift up thy hands toward him for the life of thy young children... – Lamentations 2:19a

There have been times in our family where we found ourselves in "stretching" moments with our teenage children. There have even been "stretching" seasons! Whew, Lord help all the mamas out there. Now putting them in a head lock may or may not have crossed my mind during that time, ahem. During one particular "stretching" moment, it felt like a battle. I was very frustrated over the battle I was in with that child-- frustrated at my negative responses, lack of love and compassion that I KNEW I should have had but was clearly absent. Then it hit me, "Laurie you can either battle WITH your children or battle FOR them!"

I don't want to battle with them, but if I'm not careful, that's exactly what I'll do. Here are a few lessons I've learned to keep myself on the same side of the battle line as my kids.

I.   **Walk in the Spirit**

Spending time with my Redeemer through prayer and daily Bible meditation is an incredible source of strength and wisdom for my daily journey. Galatians 5:16 says, *This I say then, Walk in the*

Spirit, and ye shall not fulfill the lust of the flesh.
Without the working of the Holy Spirit in my life, I
cannot be the mother I know I should be. I can't
respond the way I should. My flesh is just way too
stingy, ugly, and an unruly thing! With every new
stage my child enters, I am in uncharted waters. I
truly need Him!

II. Strengthen the Parent/Child Relationship

Have you heard this statement, "rules without
relationships, breeds rebellion"? Understand Satan
will do anything to destroy "key relationships."
Strengthening relationships puts us on the same
side of the battle. How can we do this?

- **Engage Your Kids**
  Do you really "know" your kids? Do you know their
  hearts? My kids are getting older and, with their
  crazy schedules, I must fight harder to make
  engagement a priority. We've seen that it's easier
  for them to come to us about issues they're dealing
  with because of the relationships we've built.
  When we sense something is wrong and they are
  silent, a gentle conversation will usually open
  those doors. This helps us guide and pray for them
  better. So many "things" can rob us of this time.
  Social media, Pinterest, hobbies, Netflix etc. These
  are not bad in and of themselves, but are we
  disengaged because of our phones? You will never
  regret spending quality time with your kids.

- **Have a Grace-Filled Home**
  Your kids are growing, changing and learning
  daily. They will not always get it right. Do you

allow grace for growth? Sin will have consequences but should always come from a heart of love for their well-being. Grace isn't overlooking an offense, it is showing love in spite of it.

We have been heartbroken by certain decisions our kids have made, but that didn't change our love for them. They need to know that our love isn't based on their behaviour, but on our positional relationship. Isn't that Gods character toward us? While one of my kids was facing a consequence for a very bad decision, we asked, "What do you need from us?" Through heavy weeping the response came, "Just love me." We could have stood in judgement and yelled about how foolish it was. Instead we chose to weep, love, and walk through it with that child. We chose to battle for, not against our child. Romans 5:20b says, *but where sin abounded, grace did much more abound.* A grace-filled home is less about behavior modification and more about heart transformation.

- **Be Approachable**
  Like us, our kids have unique personalities, different gifts, wants, and desires. Is your home an environment in which your kids can openly talk with you, or do they shut down quickly? If they feel like they can't talk to you, they won't. It's that simple! My kids have let me know when I have hurt them. Even though I may have felt they were being overly dramatic, I listened and didn't rebuke them for their feelings. That opened the door for deeper conversations. Satan will use any situation to divide. I've worked hard at being approachable.

I wasn't always this way and it really hurt my relationship with my kids. Our kids want to be heard without criticism. If they disagree, they want the freedom to express it without hostility. Meditating on Proverbs 18:13 and Proverbs 15:1 will help you gain perspective.

III. Lastly, Battle for Them!

- **Battle on our Knees**
  Hebrews. 4:16, *Let us therefore come boldly unto the throne of grace, that we may obtain mercy, and find grace to help in time of need.*

  Battling in prayer happens when I see an edgy attitude and I know something isn't right. It's there when they've been wounded by a friend or someone they admire. It's there in their consequences. It's there when they're confused and struggle to see Gods truth. It's there when their faith waivers. It's there when they have great faith but are in the valley. It's there when they choose the wrong thing. It is a great weapon against our enemy!

  My prayers can be a line of defense for my children, as the wicked one throws those fiery darts! Through a contentious spirit am I adding more darts to the arsenal? I've seen prayers save my children from bad decisions, bring them out of confusion, and more.

- **Prepare Them:** Deuteronomy 6:6-9
  Training our children with the Word of God can give them the arsenal and shield for the battle!

Oftentimes we know what God's Word says, how to handle the Word, yet we ASSUME they do too. If we haven't taught them, they won't know. Training is an everyday task. In the Bible the word training is often used in a military sense. It's a daily, repeated preparation. As with us, there's a learning curve. Recently my daughter called me from college struggling with a situation, and we went straight to God's Word. By doing so I personally gave her ammunition to deal with the situation. This built her faith and brought God's Living Word to her. As she chose to apply the Word in her own situation, Satan's lies faded and her faith grew greatly. I literally handed her an arsenal of truth with which to fight spiritual battles. Use every teaching moment you can. Good and bad ones.

Why battle with your kids, when you can battle for them?

Daily Tip:
We're in a spiritual battle daily for our kids and our families. Be willing now to fight for your kids. I see the importance of a strong relationship with them. This doesn't guarantee that things will be perfect, far from it. Give yourself grace in the areas where you've messed up. These little lessons I shared came from messing it up a million times. Our kids are so gracious. They love with a deep love. Be willing to humble yourself when you feel the need to battle against them. Rather, battle for them. And if you mess up, you'll find that they'll forgive easily.

Oh Be Careful Little Mouth What You Say!
Tamara Weatherbee

Let no corrupt communication proceed out of you mouth, but that which is good to the use of edifying, that it may minister grace unto the hearers. - Ephesians 4:29

Growing up I can remember what most of my spankings were for— "Tamara, think before you speak." It must have happened a lot because I have the worst memory.

So fast forward: my first daughter, Kenna, was just a baby. My husband would tell me ALL THE TIME, "Babe be careful; she can hear you," and of course I would reply, "Honey, she can't even talk!" Now these weren't cuss words or anything like that but small words when I would get frustrated words like dumb, ugly, idiot, I'm gonna kill you, (that is a southern phrase so don't think I'm crazy) and so on.

Fast forward a little more: our pastor was leaving our house (he happens to be my brother-in-law) and Kenna climbed up to the window with the biggest smile on her face waving and said, "BYE IDIOT!"

My husband, Anthony, and I just froze and looked at each like, "Oh, boy!" We kind of chuckled and said, "Ok, don't say that anymore." Not very sternly because we were so caught off guard. A couple weeks later we had a yard sale. As someone was leaving, Kenna again said, "Bye idiot!" We grabbed her quickly and said,

"Nooooo!" but she just kept saying "No, bye idiot!!" even louder.

You laugh now but you should have been there! That person will probably never come around this neck of the woods again!

I read a statistic that women say around 20,000 words a day, and I started to wonder what kind of words I was using. Were a majority of them positive or negative? Did you know that when we use negative or hurtful words toward or around our kids it can affect their emotional and social development? They will repeat that behavior toward those around them, which becomes a vicious cycle. We carry a lot of power with our words. But they aren't "just words." They are seeds we are planting in not just our children, but also in those around us.

We need to use the power of our words wisely. Use them to build up, not tear down.

Ephesians 4:29 says, *Let no corrupt communication proceed out of you mouth, but that which is good to the use of edifying, that it may minister grace unto the hearers.*

We have the ability to speak life or death into those around us. Something as small as a tongue has the ability to push people to greatness or to cut them like a sharp knife. We need to speak life over our kids, our friends and family. When our words match God's, our lives and the lives of those around us take on a new shape. So today, choose to speak words filled with life and watch how your day changes.

Trust me, I struggle with this daily. And I'm reminded every time I hear that little voice in the backseat of the car yelling out to my husband "faster babe!" that she is always listening.

Week Five

ENCOURAGEMENT FROM WOMEN

The Little Dids
Donna Wilson

*Now there was at Joppa certain disciple named Tabitha,
which by interpretation is called Dorcas; this woman was full
of good works and almsdeeds which she did.* - Acts 9:36

*All The Woulda-Coulda-Shouldas
Layin' In The Sun,
Talkin' 'Bout The Things
They Woulda-Coulda-Shoulda Done...
But All Those Woulda-Coulda-Shouldas
All Ran Away And Hid
From One Little Did.*

~Shel Silverstein, American poet and songwriter (1930-1999)

When I was a kid, my dad was raising my sister and me
on his own. Dad was the kind of guy who wore jeans
and flannel shirts, worked with wood and preferred
sleeping under the stars. He was raising two girls to do
the same. We ate stew almost every night, because
meat, potatoes, and carrots are good for your eyes, and
it was easily made in a crock pot. In his creative nature
he named our stew something different every night, Pot
roast, New England broiled dinner, meat and potatoes,
etc., so it took us a while to catch on. He was a sixth-
grade teacher at a Christian school. He worked hard
and in his free time was building us a house with every
penny he could scrape together. My dad loved the Lord

and worked at raising us in a godly home. In the mornings he would be seen reading his Bible, whistling hymns, and every Sunday we went to church together. Even though it was hard to be a child of divorce, I have some of the best memories of that time.

I can look back on my early years and recall fond memories with my dad, but I also have wonderful memories of certain women who had such an impact on my life during that time. These certain women helped my dad tremendously and in doing so left a lasting impression on me to the extent that when I became a mom myself I realized even more what a blessing they were in my life. There was a homeschool mom who watched us after school and during summers. Her children were more like siblings than friends. A teacher from school would also watch us, do our hair and make sure to buy us matching dresses for holidays or special events. We never missed a mother-daughter event at our church because of a sweet widow lady who would bring us or have a single lady sit with us. Looking back, I realize that was probably her match-making strategy. I had Sunday school teachers who invested in us, helping us with manners at mother-daughter events so we didn't look like cave women. Funny story, when that Sunday school teacher gently told me to get my feet off the table and sit like a lady in church I remember snapping back "You're not my mom!" A year later my Dad married her and I have had the best bonus mom and friend for the last 30 years.

These were woman who had families of their own, who worked, who had ministries and responsibilities, and chose to minister to my family. They gave of their substance by loving on two messy-haired girls and their father. Not only did they meet the physical needs in our lives, but they also met spiritual needs. They prayed for us, invested in us, played hymns on a piano during nap time, sat with us in church, pointed us to a God Who loves us and cares for us. They were love in action, in word and in deed. It was never anything big or extravagant. It was a lot of "little dids" that left a lasting impact. I love these ladies, some are in heaven, some are still here, and they are forever in my heart.

Acts 9:36 tells us a story of one such lady who had an impact on her community through her deeds. *Now there was at Joppa certain disciple named Tabitha which by interpretation is called Dorcas; this woman was full of good works and alms deeds which she did.* (Definition of Alms: anything given gratuitously to relieve the poor, as money, food, or clothing, otherwise called charity. Definition of deeds: That which is done, acted or effected, an act.) When she died these women surrounded Peter to show him all the things she had made for them and blessed them with. I love that is says "which she did," she wasn't just talk, she did!

There was a group of certain women that followed Jesus' ministry giving of their substance (Luke 8:1-3). Each of us has a different treasury from which to give. For some it's monetary, for some it's time, or homes. Whatever it is we all have a substance that we can minister from.

James 2:17-18 *Even so faith, it if hath not works, is dead, being alone. Yea, a man may say, Thou has faith, and I have work: shew me thy faith without thy works, and I will shew thee my faith by my works.*

Our homes, our churches, our schools and our communities need us to minister of our substance. We all have something to give, some way to let the Lord use us to have a lasting impact on others. Invite someone over for dinner, buy clothes for a needy family, offer to help out a single parent, teach a Sunday school class, greet a new visitor, open your homes and your hearts to someone and let them see the Love of Jesus through your deeds. I am thankful for a Dad that loved me and taught me to love Jesus, and I am thankful for the women who involved themselves in our lives and ministered to us. Like Dorcas, may it be said of us, she was "full of good works and almsdeeds which she did. " And look what a difference it made in a life. May people see Jesus through our "Little Dids."

| DAY 22 |

A Few Lessons on Being a Stepmom
Becky Card

Shew me thy ways, O LORD; teach me thy paths. Lead me in thy truth, and teach me: for thou art the God of my salvation; on thee do I wait all the day. - Psalm 25:4-5

The journey of being a stepparent has not been easy but it has been very rewarding. Many times you find yourself in a thankless job. A job where you do all the work and another person gets all the credit. If that's you, I totally understand. Thirty-four years ago it was not a common journey, but today the chances of you or someone around you being in a blended family are high. Here are a few thoughts that might encourage you if you are that mom.

You are not "mom" and that is OKAY! The children have a mom. You are not in the home to replace their mom or to circumvent their mom. Learning to view my position or place in our home as an "older woman" was a game changer! It allowed me to focus on training the children, and it took the focus off of me and my desire to be "mom."

Now, I must say it is okay to grieve the loss of that title. Many little girls dream of becoming a mom when they grow up, I was no different. It is all that I wanted to be, but God saw fit to fill my heart with many children…none of whom is my blood. It's hard, and I wish I could say I'm okay with that, but I truly believe that some day Jesus will let me know why I was chosen to be a stepmom and adoptive mom.

So, what was my position in our blended family? My place in our family was to show my daughters and my son what it means to be a God fearing wife. I am to live out in front of them a godly marriage and family. Here are my top five goals.

• Make all decisions in light of Scripture.
Prayer, quiet times, and worship (weekly church attendance and small groups) Don't talk about it ... do it! Model it!

• Life is about Relationships!
I went to the wall when the girls would speak disrespectfully to their father. It just isn't allowed. Remember, we are training children for future relationships. Learning to communicate with each other takes work and time. I'm a firm believer in how daughters ought treat their fathers and sons their mothers. It is how they will treat their spouses someday.

• Major on the majors, minor on the minors!
Now, what happens when everything feels like a major? How do you decide? Here is a little question I ask myself.... "Will it matter in 10 years?" It just seems to bring clarity to my thoughts and actions.

• Stay focused on Jesus!
We all serve an audience of ONE! After Jesus comes your husband. I LOVE being married! Instead of focusing on what isn't happening, focus on what is!

Decorate your bedroom! It should not be the last room decorated. After 34 years of marriage I would say this is key. If life is good in your marriage, the family part falls into place. Be "present" for your husband. Speak his love language. Etc.....

• **Give an endless amount of love.**
You never run out! Since this is true... encourage your children to love and respect the parent not living with you. Again, it is not a win or lose situation. I wanted the girls' mom to be treated the way I would want to be treated. Our job is to train them how to honor each other. It is NOT easy, but it is what Jesus has called us to do.

I would love to say that my blended family is walking as a unit, but that would not be true. Divorce, death, and other tragedies bring hurt and pain. Some of them can be healed quickly while others will need lots of time. So, I will continue to love and serve knowing that Jesus is faithful.

| DAY 23 |

Dear Tired Mom...
Ashley Webster

And she said, As the LORD thy God liveth, I have not a cake, but an handful of meal in a barrel, and a little oil in a cruse: and, behold, I am gathering two sticks, that I may go in and dress it for me and my son, that we may eat it, and die. And Elijah said unto her, Fear not; go and do as thou hast said: but make me thereof a little cake first, and bring it unto me, and after make for thee and for thy son. For thus saith the LORD God of Israel, The barrel of meal shall not waste, neither shall the cruse of oil fail, until the day that the LORD sendeth rain upon the earth. And she went and did according to the saying of Elijah: and she, and he, and her house, did eat many days. And the barrel of meal wasted not, neither did the cruse of oil fail, according to the word of the LORD, which he spake by Elijah. - 1 Kings 17:12-16

Dear Tired Mom,

I see you. I know those lines and that furrowed brow. I know those red eyes and that foggy brain. From a mom who is kinda on the other side- it's gonna be okay. Stop worrying about tomorrow and live right now.

Lovely Mama, God did actually make you for this. I cannot count how many times I thought, "I am not made for being a mother." The Lord proved me wrong over and over. Sometimes that baby will throw fits and embarrass you. Sometimes you will look around your house and feel as though you are drowning. It's okay. Breathe and take a step back. See it for what it is. Those dishes help provide nourishment and those clothes provide warmth. Those floors will still be dirty tomorrow and no one cares right now what your hair looks like.

Use social media sparingly and spend the day reveling in motherhood. Know that this identity is one of the most important, being a child of God. The way you rest in Him is the way those babies rest in you. You don't have to be "God" to care for them in a perfectly imperfect way. He will strengthen you for the day.

I often think of the widow woman whose oil and meal never ran out. I don't believe she was given "bulk" amounts of those things; I believe she was always given just enough for the day. She had to rest in God. She had to trust Him at His Word. What a testimony when every morning she lifted the lid and there was the same amount of meal that was there the day before.

The ONE thing I have learned from being mom to 5 kiddos is that I need His strength because mine doesn't even last past the morning routine. I need to rely on and rest in Him to be the mom HE desires me to be. Turn your eyes upon Jesus, because looking around at the laundry and the fighting and the mess is discouraging, but looking to Him gives us strength for the day. His mercies are new every morning and I believe it's especially true for mothers. Fight for those babies in your prayer closet. Fight for their futures and their innocence. Fight those overwhelming battles on your knees and they will become increasingly smaller.

Someday they won't be babies. Someday, they may

even break your heart. There is no deeper pain other than losing them completely. So be the godly mom. Be one who trusts in Him with all your heart and don't lean on your own understanding. Acknowledges God at every turn and give Him thanks always for all things! Give your kids an attitude to emulate. Show them the disposition you want to see in them. We can model bad behavior easier than good, so make conscious decisions every day. The moments are fleeting but your Savior is not. So tired Mama, go to sleep. Rest in your loving Heavenly Father's arms and know that this is HIS plan for you and these babies are your greatest contribution to the world.

| DAY 24 |

The Overwhelmed Life
Emily Lawson

If any of you lack wisdom, let him ask of God, that giveth to all men liberally, and upbraideth not; and it shall be given him. But let him ask in faith, nothing wavering. For he that wavereth is like a wave of the sea driven with the wind and tossed. - James 1:5-6

Do you ever feel overwhelmed by life? The to-do list that is never ending, the sickness that seems to be holding on to your family, the family member dealing with chronic illness, turmoil overseas...We often don't know how to handle each situation!

James 1:5-6 says, *If any of you lack wisdom, let him ask of God, that giveth to all men liberally, and upbraideth not; and it shall be given him. But let him ask in faith, nothing wavering. For he that wavereth is like a wave of the sea driven with the wind and tossed.*

God has an abundance of wisdom He wants to share with us!

Do you lack wisdom?

1. ASK!
God wants us to cry out to Him for help.

2. ASK GOD!
Our source of help is from GOD!

James says God will give to all men liberally, and he gives without reproach, which means there is no disappointment or disapproval. He isn't upset that we are asking for wisdom again. We should be encouraged that we have a generous God!

So often we turn to our friends or support groups before we turn to God. When trials come, do you grab your phone or do you pray first?

3. ASK GOD in FAITH!
James gives warning that we shouldn't waver in our request. He explains in verse 6 of chapter 1 that if we don't ask in faith, we shouldn't expect to get what we are asking for! We must grow in our faith in order to grow in our wisdom!

In what areas of your life do you need wisdom? Here is a short list I made for myself. I would encourage you to make a list of your own.

- Training my children
- Preparing junior church lessons
- Marriage relationship
- Work decisions
- House chores (how to prioritize!)
- Hospitality (how to use my home and resources)
- Health
- Church involvement

Our lives are full of situations that need wisdom. Let's not rely on our own understanding and strength. Let's be women who daily ask God, in faith, for His wisdom!

The Day After Mother's Day
Lysandra Osterkamp

She looketh well to the ways of her household, and eateth not the bread of idleness. - Proverbs 31: 27

The alarm goes off and the sun isn't even up. No breakfast in bed today. No cute little picture of my babies and me cuddled up under a flowering tree. No sweet handmade cards or flowers. Today isn't a day off from cooking, cleaning, and work. Today is a regular day. Mother's Day is over, and it feels like it will be another year until I'll feel appreciated again.

Back to reality. Back to the salt mines of laundry, chaperoning, and refereeing. Back to work. Mother's Day was yesterday, but it already feels like it was months ago. The feeling of disappointment is present in my mind as I go about my day. A part of me wishes every day were Mother's Day.

Then I watch my children playing in the back yard. My daughter twirls in circles in the sunlight as she watches her dress flow. My children are content. They have joy. They are safe, happy, and healthy. They don't have a worry in the world. They are carefree because I allow them to be carefree. I handle the things they cannot. They don't worry about whether or not they have clean clothes. They don't even think about if they'll have enough food to eat. They don't give a thought to danger. That's my job. I get to care for them, to protect them.

My children are comfortable. They have a lovely childhood. I see their delight. Their joy brings me joy. Their pleasure renews my happiness.

I'm reminded of the fact that these little ones are a wonderful gift from God to be cherished. I remember how much I love taking care of them. I love working for them. Serving them is a blessing. I don't do what I do for the thanks, the cards, or for the flowers. I do what I do for them because I love them. They are my gift from God, and I am His honored steward. Being their mom is a great privilege.

May I never lose sight of the blessings my children are. May I never take these little ones for granted. May I never forget why Mother's Day is special to me; it's because of my children. May I be the kind of mom who loves selflessly all year long.

Week Six

ENCOURAGEMENT FROM WOMEN

Stay for Long, Mama
Rachel Wyatt

Be still, and know that I am God: I will be exalted among the heathen, I will be exalted in the earth. – Psalm 46:10

My three-year-old daughter would often do something that would break my heart. When she was in the middle of trying to tell me something and I would turn my focus away from her and start absently-mindedly say "uh-huh" to her never-ending prattling, she would reach up and place her little hands, the dimpled knuckles still showing the last bits of baby fat, on both of my cheeks and turn my face toward hers.

With those beautiful, large brown eyes boring straight into my soul she would say, "Stay for long, Mama." In her childish way, she was saying, "Focus on ME, mom. Not your cooking, not whomever or whatever is on your phone, not all the other things that you feel are pressing and needing your attention, but ME.

Please don't turn away from me when I am telling you something. It may not seem important to you, but it is very important to me. Please, Mama, stay for long."

In my mind I know what the important things in life are…among the very most important is the raising of the four precious little humans that God has entrusted to my care, but how often I let other things take precedence over them! I get it, Mama. We are exhausted from being pulled in every direction by everyone all.

day. long. Our older children also are yearning for their Mama to "stay for long" and show interest in what they are doing.

Outwardly, they may come across as cool and uninterested, but inwardly they are still little children crying out for the attention and affection of their mother.

Stay for long, Mama, with that teenage daughter and let her tell you all about her drama with her friends. Take her shopping or let her help you in the kitchen as you chat about what is going on in her life. Kick a soccer ball around in the yard with your son, take interest in his newest hobby, and let him know how proud you are of him. They need you, Mama. They need your attention!

We have all had older women look at us with longing in their eyes as we are wrangling a screaming toddler into their car seat and say, "Enjoy these years…they will be gone before you know it." We utter a desperate sigh because we know what they are saying is true, but how does that translate into our frazzled, exhausted days?!

I had a conversation with my sister a couple of years ago that was a "lightbulb" moment for me. We were discussing how hard it was –as mothers– to keep up with everything with several small children, and she said, "You know…I don't think we were created to manage all that mothers today are trying to manage."

You think about mothers of past generations. They

worked hard, yes, but their lives were so much simpler. They were not trying to keep a large, multilevel home clean and organized with rooms full of toys and "things" that we have today. They weren't managing a complex schedule of sports, community, and church programs for their families. And they certainly didn't feel responsible to keep everyone that they had ever known updated on the daily happenings of their lives while at the same time consuming all the information of the daily happenings of the hundreds of friends, family, co-workers, and other random acquaintances! We were not created to be able to handle this emotional and mental workload!

I am not saying that all of these things are "bad," but I am saying that we all probably could cut back quite a bit (okay a lot!) on some of these things. Want an immediate wake-up call?! Just take a look at the screen-time history log of your phone! Am I the only one who thinks that screen-time is somehow rigged? I mean, there is no way possible that I spent THAT much time on my device!

Rigged or not, I am sure that I spent more time than I probably should have browsing, chatting, and watching. All of those minutes and even hours are ones that I could have spent "staying for long" and focusing on my family. Or perhaps it is the madness of our social schedule that needs readjusting. Maybe we need to cut down on all the material things that fill our houses and keep us running all day long to just keep up with the mess.

Fifteen years from now, it will not matter one bit if you

had the time to scroll through your Facebook feed today or watch that Netflix show, but it certainly will matter if you "stayed for long" with your children.

I know that there will come a day when I sit quietly in a rocking chair or perhaps a wheelchair and long for the days that my children were at home -- those crazy, hectic, busy wonderful days. My heart will yearn to hear their voices call me on the phone or knock at my door. Then it will be my turn to beg them to "stay for long." Stay and talk with me. Show me pictures of my grandchildren and great grandchildren, tell me about your life. I hope that I have the grace to pour my focus and attention into them now so they, in turn, will do the same for me when I so badly need them.

Whatever needs to be purged from our lives will be worth it so that we can "stay for long" with our children -- so we can focus more of our attention on them. These days are fleeting. They will soon be gone. We only have a short amount of time to "stay for long." Let's fill another sippy cup, wipe another syrup-smeared face, listen to another round of "Baby Shark" for the millionth time, prepare another snack, kiss another ouchie, listen to another dream, sooth another heartache, raise another child. "Stay for Long, Mama"…because they certainly will not.

Although our small children might be the ones that are "screaming" for our attention, our husbands and our God are also craving fellowship with us. I wonder how many times my husband has wanted and needed my attention whether physically or emotionally, and I was too busy or distracted with something else. Although he may not vocalize it, inwardly he is crying, "Stay for long, Honey." Please put down your phone and talk with me, snuggle with me, focus on ME! I am ashamed to think of how many times my Savior has wanted to say "Stay for long, child" as I hurriedly rushed through my morning devotions and scurried off to the next pressing matter. The Creator of the universe, my Savior, craves MY attention. He desires me to talk with Him, to tell Him my worries, my needs, my wants. He wants me to come to Him and pour out my heart and watch Him lift my burden.

He longs for me to read His life-giving Words that will breathe peace into my frazzled soul. But, instead, I hurry through my time with Him and rush off again, all the while wondering why I am so filled with anxiety. I can hear His soft whisper saying, "Just stay for long, child."

The Blessings of Obedience
Barbara Redlin

And the word of the LORD came unto him, saying, Get thee hence, and turn thee eastward, and hide thyself by the brook Cherith, that is before Jordan. And it shall be, that thou shalt drink of the brook; and I have commanded the ravens to feed thee there. So he went and did according unto the word of the LORD: for he went and dwelt by the brook Cherith, that is before Jordan. - 1 Kings 17:2-5

Today's thoughts come from 1 Kings 17. Imagine with me for just a few minutes...(in my mind I can see this as if it were a movie).

Elijah has just told Ahab there's going to be no rain for "these years."

--God tells Elijah to run
--Hide by the brook Cherith
--Drink from the brook and the ravens will feed you!

Elijah obeys.

--Ravens feed him bread AND flesh
The brook dries up. God again gives him instruction.
--Go to Zarapheth
--a widow woman will sustain you (this woman was a foreigner from Jezebel's home territory; God commanded her to help him)
--she's at the gate of the city gathering sticks for her & her son's last meal

--Elijah (the prophet) asks for water
--as she's going to get the water he adds, and can you
also bring back a morsel of bread (I imagine her eyes
either getting wide with fear, or she begins to cry)
--she lets him know that she doesn't have a cake/bread
but only a handful of meal and a little oil

--Elijah says, "Fear not, go & do as thou hast said..."
(make the fire, bake the little bread) BUT make mine
first! And then AFTER, make yours, BECAUSE the
LORD God of Isreal says, "the barrel of meal shall not
waste, neither shall the cruse of oil fail until the day that
the LORD sendeth rain!"

She obeyed.

--"they ate many days."
--"after these things" the son fell sick & died
--she asked Elijah, "what have I to do with thee, O thou
man of God? (again, crying maybe, anger,
exasperated...) Art thou come unto me to call my sin to
remembrance, and to slay my son? (Elijah's possibly
thinking, WOW, you're blaming me for all of this???)

--"Give me thy son."
--Elijah cries to the LORD, "Oh LORD my God, hast
thou also brought evil upon the widow with whom I
sojourn by slaying her son? (did Elijah wait for an
answer? But no reply?)
--So Elijah keeps praying...3 TIMES he asks, "Oh LORD
my God, I pray thee, let this child's soul come into him
again."

--"AND THE LORD HEARD THE VOICE OF ELIJAH"

and He said yes this time and revived the child.
--Elijah carries him back downstairs to Mom.
--She says, NOW I know because of this that you're a
man of God and that the "word of the LORD in thy
mouth is truth."

SOOOO many aspects to ponder in this snippet of
history but the main ones that struck me are these:

1. Elijah obeyed.

His obedience allowed him to receive a miracle (I have
never been fed by birds, let alone a raven)

2. The widow obeyed.

Her obedience allowed her little family bottomless meal
and oil and life, (even after her son's life was gone)
"Miracles seem so out of reach for our feeble faith. But
every miracle, large or small, begins with an act of
obedience. We may not see the solution until we take
the first step of faith." (Life Application Study Bible
notes)

God Always Blesses Obedience!

Discipling Your Child's Heart
Hollie Vaughn

When I call to remembrance the unfeigned faith that is in thee, which dwelt first in thy grandmother Lois, and thy mother Eunice; and I am persuaded that in thee also. Wherefore I put thee in remembrance that thou stir up the gift of God, which is in thee by the putting on of my hands. For God hath not given us the spirit of fear; but of power, and of love, and of a sound mind. - 2 Timothy 1:5-7

Mommas we have only one chance with our babies. There are no do-overs. We must make the most of what time and energy we have.

We hear the word discipleship preached in our churches, especially in regards to new believers.

How much time do you invest in discipling your children. It should be our first job to nurture their relationship with God. Having a heart knowledge of Jesus and not just a head knowledge.

We see a perfect example of this love for discipling in Lois and Eunice towards Timothy.

Timothy's mother and grandmother must have spent a lot of time teaching Timothy about their faith in Jesus. Paul calls it unfeighned faith. The word UNFEIGNED means not counterfeit; not hypocritical; real; sincere; as unfeigned piety to God; unfeigned love to man.

Their faith in God was real. I am not sure about you, but I've met people that are fake. Sometimes I am the person who is fake. Even Christian people struggle with being real all the time. They pretend to have it all together, but the evidence is clear that they are not as they appear.

It is hard to be fake around your children. They see you for whom you are all the time. They know if you are genuine in your love. They know if you are hypocritical in your rules. They know if you are sincere in your walk with the Lord. THESE LADIES WERE! And they passed that on to their son/grandson, Timothy.

We invest our children in sports, education, 4-H, theatre, and much more, but are we investing ourselves in them? Are we giving them our relationship with Jesus? Is it evident that we our pouring our faith into our children?

It's sad to see many Christians have a flock of people that they have won to the Lord, discipled, and have a relationship with and we see our children walk away. Why do we think that is? We have given more time to the ministry of others than to our children. They should be our greatest ministry.

I want to end by saying that I am not opposed to church discipleship. It is a command that has been given to us as Christians. What I am saying is don't get so caught up in life that you miss the most precious and valuable disciples you have in front of you all day, everyday.

The heart of discipleship is love. There is no love like a mother's love. Pass it on to your children.

Oh Be Careful Little Eyes What You See
Rachel Reed

Marriage is honourable in all, and the bed undefiled: but whoremongers and adulterers God will judge. - Hebrews 13:4

If you grew up in church, the melody to the song, "Oh Be Careful Little Eyes What You See," is probably familiar to you. Unfortunately, the message is pretty vague. It doesn't give an adequate explanation of "what could be seen."

We must tell our children what porn is. They need to know the kind of things they should be careful about seeing.

You may be a very proactive parent, guarding every movie, every device, every internet blocker...but what about the times they are not at your side? Maybe they'll be at a friend's house or at school and another child shows them something on their device, or in a magazine.

What then?

It's impossible to keep them from seeing billboards, magazine racks at grocery stores, or commercial ads for an upcoming movie. Impossible.

We come from a generation that didn't talk enough

about the dangers of pornography, but then also kept open displays of affection behind closed doors.

Both have been harmful because it gives children a perverted view of God's plan for married couples to produce a "godly seed" Malachi 2:15.

We can't leave little children to try to put together the pieces of sexual intimacy in their innocent minds because they'll stumble upon the broken pieces of an entirely different puzzle...Satan will make sure of that. Below are a few topics parents should discuss with their children:

1. Tell your kids what porn is.

2. Tell them that it may make them feel good to watch it (they need to know that...because one aspect of God's design for sex is pleasure).

3. Teach them that watching porn is the Enemy's way of pulling them into a sin addiction.

4. Teach them the basics of what sex involves. Talk to them about masturbation before their friends or teachers do. (If strangers are teaching our children about these practices in schools, we should be willing to be the proper resource as parents.)

5. Talk about marital sex and God's design for intimacy between a husband and wife. Tell them it is beautiful to God and amazing in a marriage. Let them see you kiss and hug your spouse. It's a small window for them to view affection between husband and wife in a healthy

way.

6. Be open to answer crazy, bizarre and hilarious questions! Then answer them casually, as if it's the most normal thing in the world!

7. Ask your children if they've seen anything sexual in a book, on a commercial, on a friend's device, or in a movie. Ask them often. Be specific. If they have, talk about it. Thank them for trusting you with their thoughts. Tell them about things you have seen or experienced that would relate with them. Relating with children is so healthy.

8. Assure them that they are not at fault for the things they see (temptation), but dwelling on and looking for more becomes sin. (This is important that they not have guilt from seeing something. Guilt and conviction of sin are two very different things and often confused.)

9. As a parent, live above this. Don't watch movies with pornographic images in them. Don't read novels that stir up your thought life in the wrong way.

I recently read a book with a testimony of a pastor's wife who had struggled in this area for many years as a young adult and even into her marriage. She grew up in a very protective home, but was lured into sexual sin from one encounter outside her home.

God can always give the victory, but just like any addiction, it can take over the mind and keep you in bondage for years. It hinders you from living free in Christ.

I, too, have seen victory in this in my own life and I'm so thankful for it. God is so good.

I speak from a heart that wants to protect my children, but more than protecting and shielding, we need to teach our children how to recognize the Enemy's traps, and then build a bulwark around themselves to defend themselves. They need to know God's reward for keeping themselves pure far outweighs any reward of their flesh!

How fair and how pleasant art thou, O love, for delights! I am *my beloved's, and his desire* is *toward me.* - Song of Solomon 7:6, 10

Marriage is honourable in all, and the bed undefiled: but whoremongers and adulterers God will judge. - Hebrews 13:4

Drink waters out of thine own cistern, and running waters out of thine own well. Let thy fountains be dispersed abroad, and rivers of waters in the streets. Let them be only thine own, and not strangers' with thee. Let thy fountain be blessed: and rejoice with the wife of thy youth. Let her be as the loving hind and pleasant roe; let her breasts satisfy thee at all times; and be thou ravished always with her love. And why wilt thou, my son, be ravished with a strange woman, and embrace the bosom of a stranger? For the ways of man are before the eyes of the LORD, and he pondereth all his goings. His own iniquities shall take the wicked himself, and he shall be holden with the cords of his sins. He shall die without instruction; and in the greatness of his folly he shall go astray. - Proverbs 5:15-23

Preparation for New Adventures
Heather Teis

Go to the ant...consider her ways, and be wise...Provideth her meat in summer and gathereth her food in the harvest. Proverbs 6:6, 8

What is coming around the bend in your life? Does a new season lie ahead of you?

For some, like me, you're facing the all-too-soon departure of one of your children from the home. Whether they are leaving for a new job, college, military, or ministry, before we know it, they'll be heading out the door with overflowing suitcases and eager expectations in hand...and they'll be leaving behind rooms filled with quiet and childhood memories. This is an unsettling new reality for us moms.

As in most times with a new season approaching, I have been reading and praying; praying and reading. I don't think of myself as the laborious, prepared ant...especially when it comes to the weekly dinner menu for the family. I wish I had consistently planned our meals on a weekly basis, but alas I have not, and yet somehow we have survived.

But, in this instance, like a little sugar ant (for that is surely the kind of ant I would be), I have started trying to store up some wisdom and figure out what to do now so that those parenting tomorrows are met with preparation and success.

In my excess of reading, mostly to prepare my heart for the days ahead and to hopefully cry enough now so that I won't embarrass my son by bawling my eyes out from his graduation-to-college departure, I have found some very practical ant-like advice. One of my favorite thoughts, thus far, came from *Give them Wings* by Carol Kuykendall. (By the way, her book has been fantastic; it's got the humor, the spiritual, the practical, and all the "feels" I was looking for.)

Her fantastic tip was on making a list of things you hope to ensure that your child knows before he or she leaves home. I know that I've heard this before, and of course, isn't our entire parenting career pretty much getting them ready to follow God confidently and successfully into adulthood? So, yes, there's been preparation.

But while we've done some of this along the way, with the window of opportunity soon closing, I thought it would be a good idea to knock off a few more by getting organized. It's been surprising to me, in the journey of parenting, how many road signs I failed to point out along the way because I didn't think of it. For example, for about two months while in the sixth grade, one of my children was applying the deodorant that I had dutifully bought on the shoulders instead of on the armpits! (No wonder those sixth grade classrooms often smell so bad!)

When told how to apply the deodorant correctly, my child responded with that middle-school certainty,

"But, mom, I sweat on my shoulders."

Smh.

"Yes, dear, but you stink in your pits," I replied.

(This is the problem with this generation, they haven't had the benefit of not being able to fast-forward all those informative deodorant commercials with graphs and color-coded body charts.)

So, I could relate when a mom shared with me that her high school daughter didn't know how to mail a package at the post office. God used that little incident to encourage her to make a list of things she hoped to go over with her children before they left home.

God used her story to encourage me to do the same and I'm sharing my version here for any who have high schoolers at home. The goal of this list is not to burden you. The author didn't complete her entire list, and that was okay. The point is that we are covering the bases as best we can, preparing our child for the future, and trusting God with the rest.

Plus, all of us have had to turn to YouTube at some point in our lives to figure something out. As the author of the book mentions, "Necessity is the mother of invention." They'll find a way to accomplish what we miss, and they'll mature from that, too! One more thing, consider these as opportunities to enjoy little moments of their last year at home; it's a chance to build your relationship and spend time together.

I've included my list below for your convenience. Give yourself and your teen some encouragement by putting a few on there that they already know (or that you're pretty certain they know) so that you'll feel accomplished and be reminded of the many things they have already learned over the years! (Doesn't everyone love starting with a list that's already got some items checked off?!?!)

You'll notice a few things missing on mine:

*I did not put important, vague things here. For the most part, these are specific tasks that can be measured.

*There are some things missing such as teaching my kids, especially my girls, about physical safety and awareness in situations. This is something we continually work on, so I just didn't need to go there. If you do need to add that or other items, remember to make specific benchmark goals such as having conversation about what to do if being followed in a car or on foot, take a self-defense class with child, etc.

*The last items you'll see omitted are ones that I felt were somewhat self-explanatory or will come at a later date. (Filling out a job application and doing taxes would be two examples.)

So, for you dear moms who are walking down this same road, I hope that this clears the terrain a little. Happy trails to you, my friend!

GETTING READY FOR LIFE

COMMUNICATION
- using the post office for mailing packages
- address an envelope
- using social media
- memorize address
- memorize phone numbers of parents
- how to confidently turn down a date or any unwelcome advances

FINANCIAL
- writing checks/balancing accounts
- open a credit card account to build credit
- understand the difference between credit and debit
- explain credit cards that are not free sign ups and loans that have interest rates
- open a savings account
- have a place for important docs: birth certificate, SSN, med. and car insurance, etc.
- use an ATM to make deposits and withdrawals

HOUSEHOLD
- doing laundry
- sew a button back on
- mend a rip or hem that's come loose
- basic cooking
- plunge a toilet
- turn off water at various locations
- turn off electricity in various rooms
- wash something unusual (tennis shoes, etc)
- iron
- clean a toilet
- light the pilot light on a water heater or fireplace

- light a grill and grill something
- make a bed with clean sheets
- calling phone company or others about service issues

AUTOS and TRANSPORTATION
- changing a flat tire
- putting air in tire
- jump a dead battery
- pumping gas
- filling washer fluid
- how to use a buspass/uber/lyft
- use a paper map or atlas
- use phone directions/apple maps
- find the gate in airport connection and way through the airport

HEALTH
- basic first aid
- fill out doctor's form
- understand basic health insurance
- schedule a doctor's apt.
- how to find a doc on your insurance plan (and double check that they take your insurance when you call for apt.)

SPIRITUAL
- complete the study booklet "Dating Standards" (sold at shopironwood.org)
- learn to use a Strong's concordance
- learn to use a commentary
- learn simple gospel plan to be able to lead someone to the Lord (need, way, response)

PERSONALIZED LIST

-
-
-
-
-

Encouragement From the Men Who Encourage Us

ENCOURAGEMENT FROM WOMEN

| BONUS DAY 1 |

But if not...
Neal Berkey

If it be so, our God whom we serve is able to deliver us from the burning fiery furnace, and he will deliver us out of thine hand, O king. But if not, be it known unto thee, O king, that we will not serve thy gods, nor worship the golden image which thou has set up. - Daniel 3:17-18

Do you ever consider the Hebrew children who stood their ground in the face of death with King Nebuchadnezzar and ask yourself...Why were there only three? There were literally thousands of Hebrews who were stolen away from their homes as young teens. Some believe the girls became the wives of the heathen men. Many boys like Daniel were made eunuchs and served in the king's court. Most of them had been ripped away from their families; many probably saw their parents murdered as they were taken away into slavery. But, if there were literally thousands, why do we only hear about these three and Daniel?

I recently read the testimony of a well known singer who was raised as a Christian. Her father was a Baptist youth pastor and the majority of her extended family are Christians.

Tragedy struck their family when her older cousin, whom she admired, was suddenly killed in an automobile accident. According to the singer, her cousin was a dedicated follower of Jesus, and she couldn't get past the question of, "If God is good, why didn't He protect my cousin?" She alluded to the fact that she had been taught all her life that if you love God and obey Him, you have some sort of supernatural protection. As I continued to read, it became obvious she is still at a loss on this issue.

Her lack of the knowledge of God reminds me of the Hebrew children who bowed, the ones we don't read about in Scripture.

The three Hebrew children, no longer boys, yet not quite men, stood in the face of death when they chose to follow the commandment of the Lord and not bow down to anything other than Jehovah God.

The wording in this passage leads me to believe that Hananiah, Mishael and Azariah (also known as Shadrach, Meshach, and Abednego), were not only taught the great saving miracles of our God, but they were also taught that God doesn't always work in ways we would expect.

No doubt Hananiah's parents spoke of the miracles of their great Hebrew God when He saved David from the giant Goliath. I imagine at dinner, Mishael's father told his favorite Hebrew history story of when God saved the Israelites from the Egyptian army by miraculously parting the Red Sea. Maybe as a child, Azariah pretended to be Samson, wearing a blindfold and asking God to give him strength one last time to avenge the Lord's name.

Though undoubtedly they were well versed in the

abilities and miracles of God, they also knew the not so popular history of when Hebrew babies were ordered to be murdered by Pharaoh. They studied the plagues that hit the Egyptian households.

Today we can read and study the miraculous history of the three Hebrew children, Shadrach, Meshach, and Abednego, and be encouraged that our God can and does do great things! Praise God for that!

But...

Let us not neglect to teach our children that our great God does not always work in the way we expect. The miracle doesn't always show up to rescue us at the last minute. Continue to teach the truth that our God CAN! But if not...

These Hebrew children knew their God could do anything, yet they knew their God's ways were not always their ways.

If we are to raise children to love and know God, we need to teach them all the aspects of God, not just the ones that are appealing to us. Tragedy will strike your family, there will be heartache, there will be sorrow, there will be questions of "Is God really good?"

We can choose to answer the questions before the tragedy strikes, before they are in the battle, before they must face temptation. Teach them to know all the aspects of God, and that He is always good. Show them that His ways are not our ways...His ways are better!

Let's stop painting God as something He is not, let's stop only showing part of God's character to the little ones that we lead. When we don't teach our children to fully know God, they grow up confused and continually wonder if God is truly whom He says He is, and question His goodness…often because we have neglected to teach His full character.

Let's be like those who taught Hananiah, Mishael and Azariah to continue to stand for right even in the face of persecution, knowing that our God can and will do miraculous things… But if not…if God doesn't answer our prayers the way we expect… we will still serve only Him. He is still good.

My Mom, My Hero
Robb Redlin

My son, hear the instruction of thy father, and forsake not the law of thy mother. For they shall be an ornament of grace unto thy head, and chains about thy neck. - Proverbs 1:8-9

Before I can tell you about what a wonderful, godly mom I had the honor to grow up under, I first have to give the background of whom my dad was and what he did for a living.

My dad was a police officer and not just any police officer but a sergeant, arson investigator and an undercover drug buy officer.

That's right! My dad bought illegal drugs for a living.

Of course he would also arrest the people he bought the drugs from. He would many times be called out in the middle of the night and could be gone for several hours or several days. My mom would have no idea when he might come home or whether he was dead or alive.

I say all that to tell you how difficult this must have been on a mother with four children at home with four very differing personalities and all of whom wanted her time and attention. Let me just say that I rarely saw my mom frustrated. I never heard her complain or wallow in self-pity. She just did the things that I thought all moms did. She prayed with us, read God's Word to us. She made sure we were in Church for every service. She played with us, laughed with us, cried with us, disciplined us, and was prepared to answer all of our life questions. She came to all our school functions, came to our games, watched whom we hung out with, and did it all the way a godly Christian woman with poise and dignity would do it.

Please don't get me wrong. My dad was an amazing dad as well and I'm grateful for his godly influence on my life as well, but I am also so thankful for a Mom that so often had to parent alone but did it because she loved God and she loved her kids!

If you're a single mom or a mom that is often raising kids while your husband is at work, please remember that your calling to be a mom is so vitally important to God and to your kids. It may, at times, seem overlooked but in the long run it will be worth every second you invest in them. One day they will look back and be ever so thankful for their hero whom they have had the pleasure of calling MOM!

My Grandma's Unfeigned Faith
Aaron Wilson

I thank God, whom I serve with a pure conscience,
as my forefathers did, as without ceasing I remember you in
my prayers night and day, greatly desiring to see you, being
mindful of your tears, that I may be filled with joy, when I
call to remembrance the genuine faith that is in you, which
dwelt first in your grandmother Lois and your mother
Eunice, and I am persuaded is in you also. Therefore I remind
you to stir up the gift of God which is in you through the
laying on of my hands. For God has not given us a spirit of
fear, but of power and of love and of a sound mind. - 2
Timothy 1:3-7

I remember the first time reading these verses as a new
Christian. I couldn't believe my eyes — Timothy had a
grandma! I was biblically illiterate at the time, and it
took me awhile to understand all the people and
circumstances surrounding the letters of the NT. Paul
was writing to Timothy, a young pastor whom he had
been mentoring. Paul mentioned Timothy's godly
heritage found in his mother and grandmother. Wow!
These were real people with real families, and God was
using their family heritage to pass along their faith in
Christ. Timothy had a godly grandma and that made all
the difference!

I had just received Christ during my senior year of high
school. As God began this great work of sanctification
in me, my life changed dramatically. When I say

changed, I mean everything was changing — my friends, my weekends, my direction, my desires, my plans--- EVERYTHING! What I remember most about that time was the change in my relationship with the Bible. That old, obsolete book was becoming alive to me! I couldn't explain it at the time, but the Bible began to speak to my heart. As a young Christian, I wasn't as theologically or doctrinally astute as maybe after my Bible college training. I didn't understand concepts such as verbal-plenary inspiration, textual criticism, inerrancy, preservation, etc. However, I knew I had a book that kept speaking to my heart. And these verses about Timothy's godly grandma jumped off the page!

My childhood is filled with lots of memories of my grandma. She is a kind and thoughtful lady. She loves birding, crafting, and traveling. She loves her family and grandkids very much. She never missed one of our sports games. During autumn, we used to have bonfires with smores and hotdogs. On some of those hot summer nights, we used to lay on a blanket out in grandma's front yard, pop some popcorn and watch the bats fly above our heads. She would run around the yard with us chasing and sometimes catching lightning bugs.

Grandma had a strong faith in God, too. Grandma used to go by herself to a small Baptist church. I remember her inviting us to special meetings and Vacation Bible School. Every summer, she would have a back yard Bible club in her yard where some teacher would come and do games, sing songs, and tell stories about Jesus. I didn't remember much, except I always looked forward to the popsicles or treats afterwards. I would sit through almost anything to get a popsicle on one of those hot summer days! But the one thing I remember most about my grandma — I remember my grandmother's commitment and devotion to Jesus Christ. She would always be reading her Bible and going to church. She would sing and talk to us about the Lord. Although, I didn't receive Christ until later, this indeed had a profound impact on me.

At age 17, when I came home from a youth rally where I had gotten saved, my grandma was the first person I told. I remember it vividly. I came over to her house because I had something to tell her. We sat down at her little brown table in the basement right outside the laundry room. I told her I became a Christian and that God had called me to be a preacher. With tears rolling down her cheek, she told me that she had never stopped praying for me. She loved all her grandkids, but she sensed that the Lord had something special planned for me in His Work. She was the first to buy me a Bible and encourage me along the way. Now, after almost 20 years of being in the ministry, I look back and recognize the impact of grandma's faith in my life. Just like Timothy, my grandma's faith made a difference in my ministry.

Timothy's grandma's faith had such an impact that Paul recorded it in the Bible. What a testimony! Keep living your faith every day. Even when you do not feel it is making a difference. What you do makes a difference to God, to your family, and to those in your sphere of influence. My grandma's faith still impacts me today. She is my godly heritage. And by the way…her name is Lois, too!

Homework
Donny Wilson

Strength and honour are her clothing; and she shall rejoice in time to come. She openeth her mouth with wisdom; and in her tongue is the law of kindness. She looketh well to the ways of her household, and eateth not the bread of idleness. Her children arise up, and call her blessed; her husband also, and he praiseth her. - Proverbs 31:25-28

Seventh grade, the year I thought I was cooler than I actually was and learned my mom was pretty cool too. I loved school, not the academic parts, more like the friends and sports parts, and that clearly showed in my grades. It's not that I wasn't able or capable of doing the work, it's just that I was more motivated by goofing around and socializing. My grades revealed the flawed motivation and I was what they would call a "below average" student.

At that same time my mom had gone back to school to become a nurse. Maybe she needed the accountability, or maybe she wanted to make sure we were doing our homework after seeing a report card, but whatever her reasoning, my mom made us start sitting at the kitchen table with her to do all our homework together. I hated it. The more I fought the more she stuck to her guns. I'm sure the two young boys were more distracting than helpful in her schooling endeavors, but she kept sitting with us, encouraging us and making us complete our homework.

That simple act of her strong will versus mine, her loving steadfastness to make me get my homework done revolutionized my academic career. I'm sure it would've been easier for her to do her homework without us bugging her. The time we spent together changed my perspective about schooling and I am forever grateful. That year I went from being a below average student to getting above average grades and all I did was turn in my homework.

When I look back on this event it's barely a blip in the radar of time, but it's amazing how ingrained in my memory this event is. It really is the little steadfast loving moments in the day-to-day life of a child that make all the difference.

Thanks mom for making me do my homework, becoming a nurse, and for being lovingly steadfast, that was pretty cool of you.

Victory for The Single Moms!
Sean Teis

For the word of God is quick, and powerful, and sharper than any twoedged sword, piercing even to the dividing asunder of soul and spirit, and of the joints and marrow, and is a discerner of the thoughts and intents of the heart. - Hebrews 4:12

We all want to succeed in life! No one actually wants to fail. But how do we reach that success? As a Christian the most successful people we know are the ones that put the Bible in the central nervous system of their personal lives and homes. Parents that succeed the best are the ones that fill their homes with God!

How do we do this? In our verse today it tells us just how magnificent and important the Bible is to each and everyone of us. You might be thinking, "I've heard this verse before and how does this apply to my single mom life?"

If the Word of God was the only tool you had to succeed as a single mom, you could win! It has all the answers! It has all of the guidance! It has all of the help! It has what you need! Single moms that succeed the most have worked very hard to center their home, their personal lives, and their children's lives on God!

Why does this matter? Because when you fill your home with God, it is a lot harder for wickedness to consume your home!

For example:

- Eyes / Ears - want to protect your child's mind? Then filter what you and your children watch and listen to. Don't watch or listen to anything that you couldn't watch with God in the room.
- Friendships/ Relationships - protect yourself and your children from unhealthy friendships and relationships. If those relationships don't honor God, break them off! Your children are way more important than any other relationships!
- Money - handle money the way God tells us to with giving back at least 10% to him, not taking on bad debt, and other Bible truths on how to manage money.
- Joy - the Bible talks a lot about having joy as a Christian! Life will get you down, but let joy control your life!

See what I mean?! The Bible literally has an answer for everything, and it can help you and be your guide on your single mom journey!

How do I put this to action? What is your family going through right now? Find those verses that will help your family conquer your trials. Take those verses, paint them on a canvas, write them on a post it note, stick them on the fridge, put them in your car, or wherever your family will see and focus on them. When God has given you the stronghold on those trials and something else arises find other verses and focus on them. Overcome your families' obstacles through the

Word of God and point your children to verses during the good and bad times. But remember, when God has given you victories, celebrate them. Celebrate those moments of victory in your faith so that your children can see that God truly is their loving Dad!

An Invitation to Contribute

We at EFW are always looking for inspiring authors who seek to encourage others in their walk with the Lord.

Please visit encouragementfromwomen.com if you would like to submit a devotional that would appear on our social media accounts.

✉EFW@experienceliberty.com

⦿encouragementfromwomen

f EncouragementFromWomenWhoveBeenThere

Author Biographies
(Organized Alphabetically)

Charity Berkey
Charity is the founder of Encouragement From Women Who've Been There [EFW]. The EFW website and social media platforms provide daily biblical encouragement and resources for women around the globe. Currently the EFW social media pages actively reach over 240,000 followers. Charity resides in her hometown of Las Vegas where she and her husband, Neal, have served on staff at Liberty Baptist Church for the past eighteen years. Though she loves serving in various ministries, Charity's favorite calling continues to be her role as wife to Neal and homeschool mama to their four children, Tre, Cherish, Lincoln, and Felicity.

Neal Berkey
Neal is the associate pastor of Liberty Baptist Church in Las Vegas, Nevada. Neal was born and raised in Jacksonville, Florida. In 2006 the Lord brought Neal to work on staff as a summer intern at Liberty. It was there that he met his wife Charity. A few years later they were married and joined the pastoral staff of the church. He currently serves as the lead in their counseling, missions, and children's ministries. Since 2015 he has actively served alongside Las Vegas Metro Police Department as a police chaplain.

Laurie Billings

Laurie is a mother of four, with two NEW grandbabies she's madly in love with. She has been married for 28 years, serving joyfully alongside her sweetheart Aj, who is the senior pastor at Dupont Baptist Church in Indiana. She is a lover of all things beachy, an avid tea drinker and loves deep diving into God's Word. For encouragement you can find her over at Instagram: laurieannie_6, or on Facebook: Laurie McCann Billings.

Becky Card

Becky is a wife, bonus mom, adoptive mom and retired elementary school teacher. She is a cancer survivor. In her free time, she loves to crochet, bake, grow succulents, and volunteers in a variety of women's ministries. Becky and her husband Doug live is Hesperia, California.

Katie Chappell

Katie is a wife and mom of three kids ages eight, six, and five. In 2017, their family planted Rock Hill Baptist Church in Rancho Cucamonga, CA. God certainly is doing a great work in Southern California and it is her highest honor to serve Him alongside her family.

Faith Glosser Conaway

Faith is a single mama to 3 teenage girls living in Texas. By day, she is a small business assistant and bookkeeper. She and her girls enjoy cooking, shopping, and serving together. You can find her on Facebook at: Faith Glosser Conaway

Heather Cusumano
Heather is a wife, mom to three, designer, author of
PRAA Journal, and photoshoot producer living in
Central Pennsylvania where she loves the Fall but hates
the winter. She's super picky when it comes to food
(but loves black licorice), has random dance parties in
the kitchen with her family, enjoys all things lunch and
coffee with friends, and can't remember the last time
her hair was its natural color. She thrives on finding
solutions to problems and believes that if she lives her
life as a true Disciple of Jesus first in her home, she can
make a difference not only in the lives of her family, but
in her community and beyond. And she believes you
can, too. You can find Heather on Facebook
@PRAAjournal or visit her website:
seven38designs.com

Kaitlyn Gellos
Kaitlyn is the wife of Evangelist Brent Gellos. They,
along with their six children, make their home in
Kentland, IN. Together, they travel around the country
and world, sharing Jesus Christ. To read more about
their ministry, visit: brentgellos.com

Charisse Goforth

Charisse is a Pastor's wife from Caseville, MI. She and her husband Mike have been married for 36 years and have 4 children and 6 grandchildren. They have been involved in the ministry their entire marriage, and Mike has been the Pastor of Calvary Baptist Church in Caseville since 1994. She started her blog and Facebook page, Holding Hope, in 2016. Her desire is to be used by God to continually bring hope to women of all ages. She has a soft spot for motherhood and often writes on this topic. Charisse's children all serve in the ministry and if you were to ask her what the best advice is for young moms, she would tell you prayer. Saturate your husband, your children and your home in prayer continually. You can find her blog here: https://www.holdinghope.co/blog-home.html You can also follow her on Facebook (Holding Hope) and Instagram (@holdinghopecbc).

Jacklyn Gunner

Jacklyn is the wife of Sam Gunner and the mother to three beautiful children. God has allowed her to serve as the Pastor's Wife of Lifepoint Baptist Church in Sterling Heights, MI since 2014. She also has the wonderful privilege of teaching second grade at a Christian school. Jacklyn has seen God work mightily in directing her life from a bus kid born in Roanoke, Virginia, to a Bible college student in California, and now to a pastor's wife. She has a passion to encourage young people to surrender to God at an early age. She loves to teach the Bible, speak to ladies, and cook. You can find Jacklyn through Facebook: Jacklyn Gunner or by email: mrs.jgunner@gmail.com

Jen Helton

Jen is a missionary wife serving the Lord in Southern Spain with her husband, Michael. She loves all things coffee, fitness, and facetiming her adult children who live in the United States. Instagram: @mylife_in_spain; Facebook: Michael-Jen Helton; website: www.heltonsforspain.com

Emily Lawson

Emily and her husband, Craig, have served at Ironwood Camp in southern California since the summer of 2014. Emily is the director of Women's Ministries and the Program Team secretary. Along with camp ministry, the Lawson family is passionate about their local church. Raised in Wisconsin (Go Pack Go!), Emily has come to love the beauty and people of the high desert. Craig and Emily have two young children, Cooper and Makenna.

Sarah Link

Sarah lives in St. Marys, GA where her husband, Donald, is the Pastor of Coastal Baptist Church. They have been married and in the ministry for 15 years. She is also a homeschooling mom to 5 precious kids. Sarah and her family have seen God do the impossible during difficult trials and in turn have experienced even greater miracles. It's through those times that God has given Sarah a deep passion to counsel and encourage others to strengthen their relationship with the Lord.

Muriel Livermore
Muriel is a church planter's wife in Metro Detroit, Michigan. She homeschools her 4 kids and loves helping people learn who they are in God's perfect plan for their lives.

Katie Oatsvall
Katie and her husband Paul live in rural Wisconsin where Paul pastors a sweet country church. Together they have two long-awaited, prayed-for children, Adelynn and Bradley. Katie was born and raised in Las Vegas, Nevada. She would have never thought she'd end up in farmland, but she praises God for a heart for the Mid-West!

Lysandra Osterkamp
Lysandra is a passionate follower of Jesus. She is a speaker, storyteller, teacher, pod caster, woman's and marriage counselor, and author. She is married to her childhood sweetheart Thomas Osterkamp, Lead Pastor at Beachside Community Church, Palm Coast, Florida. They have been serving God in pastoral ministry for 18 years. Lysandra and Thomas homeschool their four beautiful, spunky, funny girls: Kathryne, Isabella, Abigail, and Violet. Their house is always busy, dramatic, exciting, and full of love. Her book, *Balancing the Crazy* is available on Amazon and kindle. Her podcasts, "Family Meeting" and "Everyday Christian Mom" can be found on most podcast providers. Please visit her website at, lysandraosterkamp.com. You can find her on Facebook at, Lysandra Osterkamp Motivational Speaker.

Nichole Rabon
Nichole is a wife and mom to three children. She has served alongside her husband at Beacon Baptist Church for the past 13 years in the youth ministry. She desires to help other ministry moms raise their children to know, love, and serve Jesus. Instagram: @nichole.rabon; Facebook: Nichole Newman Rabon; website: nicholerabon.com

Sharon Ammons Rabon
Sharon grew up in a Christian home in Midland City, Alabama. She trusted Christ as her Savior and gave her life to serve the Lord in lifetime ministry as a teenager. Sharon married her high school sweetheart, Tim Rabon, on July 27, 1997. In 1981 they were asked to join the staff of Beacon Baptist Church in Raleigh, NC. In 1997, her husband became the pastor of that church. Sharon is director of ladies' ministries and serves as her husband's secretary. She has written two 60 day devotional books entitled *Pause* and *Selah*. You can purchase both on her website, www.sharonrabon.com, as well as find other helpful resources. She is the mom of two sons and one daughter, all of whom are married and serve in lifetime ministry. Her favorite role is being Nana to eight Cute Kids.

Barbara Redlin
Barb has served over the past 27 years as a Christian schoolteacher, wife, youth pastor wife, missionary wife, Church planter wife and now lead pastor wife. She and her husband, Robb, serve at Calvary Community Baptist Church in Northglenn CO. She loves spending time with her family (Tell, Taylar and Anne'), sitting in the sun with a good book and a glass of sweet tea!

Robb Redlin

Pastor Robb Redlin has been married to his wife
Barbara for 27 years. They adopted their first child Tell
from Ukraine when he was 5. Six years later God
blessed them with their daughter Anne' who is now 15.
Robb has been in ministry for 27 years. He started out
in youth ministry outside of Chicago where he served
for eight years. Then the Lord led him and his wife
Barbara to be missionaries in the country of Wales. The
Redlands then had the opportunity to plant Mountain
View Baptist Church in Las Cruces, New Mexico. The
Lord then led the Redlin family to the Denver area
where Robb has been pastoring Calvary Community
Baptist for the last 3 years.

Rachel Reed

Rachel and her husband Nick have been involved in
pastoral ministry for more than 12 years. Nick is the
founding pastor of CityLight and has a passion to reach
Los Angeles with the gospel of Jesus. Rachel leads the
church offices, ladies ministry and helps coordinate
ladies' events. She loves interior designing commercial
and residential spaces and refinishing furniture.
Together they have four children. You can learn more
from her by following her Instagram page
@reedsindeed.

Emily Sealy
Emily lives in Canada with her husband of 16 years and her four children whom she homeschools. She and her husband were in church ministry for the first 11 years of their marriage. Emily has had a lifetime of health issues which eventually led to her losing the use of her legs and becoming a full-time wheelchair user in 2018. Emily loves to write, and uses that love to write about life in a wheelchair and the challenges that brings, as well as all that God is teaching her in day-to-day life. Her passion is to encourage others. While life may be hard, God is always good. You can read more of her writings on her blog at www.emilysealy.com.

Haley Shoemaker
Haley is a wife and mother of three. She leads a busy life divided between home and ministry. Haley and her husband have an outdoor ministry that seeks to disciple people through experiencing and enjoying God's creation. @narrowwayoutdoors

Francie Taylor
Francie is a ladies' Bible teacher, author, and founder of Keep the Heart, a teaching ministry for Christian women. Francie teaches at many ladies' Bible conferences and retreats in and out of the country. Previously from First Baptist Church of Rosemount, Minnesota, Francie now lives in Pensacola, Florida where she attends the Campus Church at Pensacola Christian College while running a busy ministry which includes traveling to conferences, writing, and recording shows for Keep the Heart Podcast.

Heather Teis

Heather is the Counseling Coordinator and Women's Ministry Director at Southern Hills Baptist Church.

Heather has served in ministry alongside of her husband Josh since their marriage in 2001. Originally from Alabama, she has since grown to love the city and people of Las Vegas. She enjoys hiking with her family, watching her kids play sports, rooting for Alabama Football, and getting alone with a good book and some chocolate. She loves serving as a counselor and coordinator for the Ladies ministry as well as assisting her husband with the various ministries at Southern Hills.

Heather also coordinates quarterly ladies events, speaks at conferences, hosts church-wide events alongside her husband, and assists in office responsibilities.

Sean Teis

Besides being a Christian the two most important responsibilities Sean has is in being the husband to his wife Jackie and the father of his three awesome children Malachi, Titus and Blaire.

Sean and Jackie started Life Factors Ministries in 2008 to spread hope to fatherless children. Their passion is to see these families set free through the hope that can only be found in a transforming relationship with Christ.

If you would like to schedule the Teis family to come to your church or event contact them at info@lifefactors.org.

Calah Vogel
Calah is a born again believer and a friend of God. She is a military wife and a mother of six children. Her passion is to encourage other wives and mothers to find practical ways to love their husbands and children. She loves Jesus, people, coffee, and chocolate. You can reach her on Instagram at vogelcalah or on Facebook at Calah Vogel.

Tamara Weatherbee
Tamara is a stay-at-home mom to her three little ones. She truly enjoys being able to stay home with her children but also work from home. She is a social media influencer where she loves to empower and validate women all over the world. Tamara and her husband, Anthony, have served at Lighthouse Baptist Church in Gulf breeze Florida where her husband has been the Assistant Pastor for 7 years. You can connect with Tamara on Instagram @tamara_weatherbee, Facebook tamara_weatherbee, Tiktok @tamara_weatherbee.

Aaron Wilson
Aaron and his wife Tina spent nine years serving at the First Baptist Church of Bridgeport, MI, where Aaron served on full time staff. While there, the Lord strengthened and grew their desire to minister to youth and families. Aaron has served as Executive Director at Camp CoBeAc since January of 2014. Tina grew up coming to CoBeAc, and has loved showing their boys, Jackson and William, all the places that hold special memories around camp. She now serves as the Office Manager and Lifeguard Trainer.

Donna Wilson

Donna has served alongside her husband, Pastor Donny Wilson, in ministry for the Last 20 years in Moreno Valley California. They have four children whom they homeschool, two tortoises and two to three dogs depending on the strays any given child has brought home. For fun, Donna likes to travel with her family, have friends over, work on different creative projects around her home, and randomly burst out into songs with made up lyrics. She loves soul shopping which is basically sharing Jesus with others while out shopping. She feels that loving Jesus is such a joy, and getting to serve him truly is a blessing.

Donny Wilson

Pastor Donny Wilson was a hick from Colorado who met a California girl at Bible College and never left California. He and his wife Donna have been serving at their church in Moreno Valley California for the last 20 years. Donny began as a youth pastor and loved working with teens until God moved him to be the lead pastor 6 years ago. In his free time Donny enjoys the outdoors, guns, and watching super hero movies with his kids. He loves serving the Lord with his family and can't imagine life outside the ministry.

Hollie Vaughn

Hollie is a wife, mother, friend, pastor's wife, writer, and speaker. She and her husband Dan have been happily married since 2003. They have been blessed with four children: Jesse, Jeffrey, Olivia, and Kamryn.

In 2004 they planted Hope's Point Baptist Church in Weston, WV. Hollie spends much of her life investing in the lives of others in her church, community, as well as other ministry wives across the country. She oversees the social media page, Ladies Prayer Advance and has written several devotional Bible-study materials. She was a founding member of the social media ministry, Simply Edify.

Aside from spending time with family, Hollie is passionate about thrifting and coffee. She owns and operates My Thrifty Mama along side her mom and grandma and enjoys her signature lavender vanilla latte from The Coffeehouse which is operated by her church

Ashley Webster

Ashley Webster is a church planter's wife, mom to 5 beautiful kiddos, and a flower truck owner. She graduated from Bible college in 2008 and has been serving the Lord ever since! Her oldest daughter has epilepsy and while its brought many challenges, its also taught her and her husband to wholly trust the Lord with everything. She is currently writing a devotional book called, *Kitchen Sink Devotionals*. It's practical advice for how to study the Bible and how to pray when you're a busy wife and mother. She is a floral designer with a flower truck business that does several weddings and pop-ups a year. All of her little girls are her assistants and she loves reaching her community through her truck filled with blooms. She is a minimalist coffee junkie with a heart for children and ministry! Her email is ashleysflowertruck@gmail.com and her social media page is Ashley Prater Webster on Facebook and ashleys_flowertruck on Instagram.

Rachel Wyatt

Rachel and her husband have been serving as missionaries to Tanzania, East Africa since 2007. God has blessed them with four beautiful children all of whom were born in Tanzania. Rachel fills her days homeschooling her children as well as keeping up with all the challenges of living in a foreign country. She assists Jerry, her husband, in the various aspects of the ministry and women's ministries. In her "spare time" she enjoys graphic design. You can learn more about their work on their website: www.wyatttanzania.com.

Additional Resources

EncouragementFromWomen.Com

Encouragement From Women Who've Been There currently has **three** different devotional books: *Encouragement For Women*, *Encouragement For Your Identity*, and *Encouragement For Motherhood*. You can find each of these encouraging devotionals on Amazon.

Teis Talks

Teis Talks: it's more than a conversation! Teis Talks is a fun conversation that provides biblical and practical application to the problems of your every day life.

Subscribe on iTunes, SoundCloud, or your favorite podcast app!

A Final Word

We as mothers often wrap up our identity in our motherhood. Moms often give so much of themselves for their children. The love, care and devotion of a mother is a direct reflection of how Jesus loves and cares for us.

Jesus cares about everyone! In fact, He cared about us so much that 2,000 years ago, He left the glory of Heaven to come to earth so that He could give us the gift of eternal life. The question is, how can we get this gift?

Have you ever told a lie, lost your temper, taken something that didn't belong to you? We all have. The Bible calls the breaking of God's law – sin. *For all have sinned, and come short of the glory of God:* - Romans 3:23

Our sin separates us from God, and must be paid for. *For the wages of sin is death; but the gift of God is eternal life through Jesus Christ our Lord.* - Romans 6:23

Now for the good news…Jesus Christ willingly was crucified, buried, and rose from the dead in order to pay for our sins. *Christ died for our sins according to the scriptures; And that he was buried, and that he rose again the third day according to the scriptures.* – 1 Corinthians 15:3-4

God allowed this because He is actively pursuing our hearts. *But God commendeth his love toward us, in that, while we were yet sinners, Christ died for us.* – Romans 5:8

Jesus desires that you be found. He offers us an eternal life in Heaven if we simply believe on Him for salvation. We demonstrate this belief by calling on Him. *That if thou shalt confess with thy mouth the Lord Jesus, and shalt believe in thine heart that God hath raised him from the dead, thou shalt be saved...For whosoever shall call upon the name of the Lord shall be saved.* - Romans 10:9, 13

If you've placed your trust in Christ after reading this you are officially part of the family of God! You have purpose, you have meaning, and you now have a future in Heaven. You may have questions and we would love to answer them. Please contact us so we can celebrate with you!

You were once lost, but now you are found! Your future is bright!

Made in the USA
Columbia, SC
07 April 2023

15023372R10089